The Gospel According to Jack

To Deliver Us from Neurosis

Jack Waddington

Printed in Victoria, BC, Canada

ISBN: 978-1-4251-3859-2 (sc)
ISBN: 978-1-4269-1405-8 (e-book)

Trafford

Publishing

www.trafford.com

North American & International
Toll-free 1 888 232 4444 (USA & Canada)
Phone: 250 383 6864 * fax 250 383 6804

United Kingdom & Europe
Phone: 44 1865 722 113 * local rate 0845 230 9601
Facsimile: 44 1865 722 868 * email: info.uk@trafford.com

Trafford rev. 6/16/2009

Acknowledgments

Jim Sauerbier, my lover for 18 years, who stood by me during its gestation and writing.

Deborah Grant, my friend and buddy, who inspired, encouraged and helped me to write this book.

Ben Akerley, who spent endless hours editing and re-editing my manuscripts and all my additions and alterations.

Table of Contents

Prologue

In 1967, an event took place in Los Angeles which led to a discovery. The discovery was Primal Pain. I contend that this is the greatest discovery ever made. This is the greatest discovery because we now know something about ourselves that we have been searching for millennia and sheds total light on why we are the way we are. This may sound audacious: my book attempts to demonstrate the validity of this claim.

The discovery of Primal Pain led to the development of Primal Theory. Primal Theory gives us an awareness of our neurotic existence in all its aspects. In this book I explain neurosis and attempt to elucidate its implications. Living with this awareness the next generations could become less neurotic, so that eventually we could return to our original feeling-full humanity.

Many of us feel deep down that there is something amiss in our lives and the world we live in, but we are not sure what it is. We have been seeking to resolve this question throughout our known history, and still floundering to find a solution.

I hope in this book to elucidate the problem and make suggestions as to how we *might* resolve it.

Introduction

Sometime around the mid-sixties I found myself having to attend a clinic in London, England for a penicillin injection. On getting the injection I suddenly felt a rush through my body and within seconds my heart was pounding so fast I felt it might burst out of my body. Then suddenly, there was a tearing sensation in the back of my neck. I fell to the floor screaming at the top of my lungs, "I'm dying, I'm dying." I didn't even know I had that kind of scream in me. I was seized with terror like I'd never known before. I had no idea what was happening to me, but knew I was in a situation of enormous vulnerability.

Within seconds, I felt that tearing sensation in the back of my neck again. The terror now mounted to a height that I didn't know was possible, let alone was happening to me. This second phase felt like I was now in some place in outer space. I was terrified and truly felt my life was on the line. I looked up at the doctor as I was being put on an examination table. His face was green and his hair was standing on end; Jesus, I thought, if that's how scared the doctor is, what the hell is going on with me? He seemed to have no idea what was going on with me. At that moment, there was another tearing sensation at the back of my neck. If the second one took me into outer space, I now felt I'd left the universe completely. I didn't believe it was possible to experience this amount of terror and live.

Then suddenly, I was a baby in my cot (crib) and could see the wall and ceiling above me. On the wall was a "Mickey Mouse" tricycle hanging over a gas bracket above the fireplace. The colors were unbelievably vivid, the taste in my mouth was unlike anything I'd known in my life's memory to that point and I was screaming for my life. Some seconds later, I was transposed to another scene where I was a baby crawling on the floor. I felt so small or rather the room felt so large. The carpet was familiar but the room wasn't. At that point the doctor was injecting me with some tranquilizer to quiet me down. I was indeed brought down from that scene to that of being outside the universe.

This incident was so devastating to me that it stayed with me for several years. Then in 1973 I picked up *The Primal Scream*. On reading the introduction, I was an instant convert. I threw the book in the air and exclaimed, "I've got it," i.e. the clinic incident now made total sense to me. I couldn't put the book down and read it in two days. After reading it, I started to read it again just to make sure I had got it right. Within another two days, I had reread it.

Part I

The Theory

The discovery I mentioned in the prologue was made by Dr. Arthur Janov, a psychologist who had been working for seventeen years in private practice in Los Angeles. After watching two of his patients in separate sessions writhing on the floor for several minutes, and listening to the recordings he made of them, Janov named this discovery "Primal Pain." He defined Primal Pain as the pain that resided within every neurotic from early childhood. This he recounted in the introduction of his famous best-selling book *The Primal Scream*.

Earlier, others had noted that pain from the past resides within us and affects us for the rest of our lives. Sigmund Freud acknowledged its presence and impact. Others had suggested that all events in our past were stored intact in our memories though they did not make clear why this was so or what their effects were. Janov had studied many related ideas, but was somewhat dissatisfied with current explanations.

On seeing his patient go through what Janov recognized as a "reliving" of a painful early childhood event, and the impact on the patient, he diligently set about, over the next several months, to explain it in psychological terms. Having a Ph.D. in neurophysiology, he was well equipped to formulate a consistent theory which has been verified both objectively and subjectively by thousands of Primal patients over the last 30 years. However, I contend the psychological profession has ignored the verification of Primal Theory by considering only the efficasy or Primal Therapy.

Primal Theory gives us an awareness of our neurotic existence in all its aspects. In part I of this book I explain Primal Theory briefly in my own words. For more details read *The Primal Scream,* and other works by Arthur Janov.

1

Neurosis

The problem

Janov defined neurosis as the pathology of feeling. When feelings are not fully accessible (a pathological condition), then we are neurotic. Freud being a neurophysician coined the word "neurosis" but did not adequately define it. Not until Janov and *The Primal Scream* was neurosis fully defined. It is the simplicity of this definition that is it's genius, for it gives us access to how the brain (mind) works.

Janov stated that we create the subconscious to store unfelt pain and intimated that all that is contained in the subconscious is unfelt pain. He further stated that if the subconscious (pain) could be relived, as opposed to remembered, it would become part of the consciousness again as it was originally. Consequently, both neurosis and many of the mysteries of the subconscious are now demystified.

The question is: How many of us are neurotic? I feel none of us escape neurosis. I contend we all know deep down there is something, but we are never quite sure what—that something is an underlying pain. Our inability to access this pain is neurosis.

2

Need

Janov stated that we are all born needing. As are all other creatures. These needs are relatively simple. Most creatures are able to follow their instincts in satisfying their own needs and caring for their young. As newborns we need to breathe, to be fed when we need nourishment, to be held, and to be kept clean and warm. We need to feel safe and develop in our own way and time. In other words: we need to be loved.

Often we humans confuse need with want. Unmet wants may produce frustration but not disastrous consequences. Unmet needs, on the other hand, are catastrophic and affect us for the rest of our lives, unless we are able to finally feel them and respond to them. Need implies that if it is unmet, we will suffer enormous consequences.

3

Pain

When needs go unmet, we feel pain. As children we feel overwhelming pain when our needs go unmet because we have little or no resources to alleviate pain. We are totally reliant on our caregivers. Babies and very young children invariably cry when they feel pain. A baby or young child crying is in pain, contrary to some notions that babies and young children cry for effect and manipulation, or worse, just as a way to breathe or let off steam. This is a tragic myth. The pain does not go away, it just gets stored in the subconscious.

4

Feelings

A feeling is a psychophysical event or sensation within our bodies. In childhood we experience many feelings and sensations. We commonly think of feelings and emotions as the same and we use the words synonymously. However, Janov made a very clear distinction between the two, and I concur with Janov' definition: An emotion is the expression of a feeling. A full-feeling event has two components: first, the physical sensation and then, the expression (emotion), the latter indicating that the mind participates in the expression. Examples of the use of these components in a full-feeling experience are: if you are pricked with a pin, the feeling is a pin prick; the emotion is usually: "ouch." Another instance would be if you feel sad (have the sensation of sadness), the response (emotion) could be to cry.

5

Memory

Our ability to remember is fundamental to our existence. Remembering experiences will determine how we react to similar events in the future. A problem arises when we don't have total access to all our memories. We can experience the loss of memory after a traumatic event—amnesia—like a horrific road accident. A traumatic experience in a child's life from an unmet need also results in amnesia of that event. Repressed memories are not totally lost to us, but to bring them back to total memory and into our consciousness is a difficult and painful process. Repression is the loss of access to all or part of a memory, but the feelings remains reverberating within our bodies until it is fully felt.

6

The subconscious

Freud used the word "unconscious" but I would rather use the word "subconscious." For me "unconscious" suggests the loss of consciousness—knocked out. I prefer to use the word "subconscious" because it denotes under the conscious level.

Our subconscious is an aspect of our total consciousness: We are aware of our consciousness, but are only subliminally aware of our subconscious. Most of us are peripherally aware of something beyond the conscious mind, but we have no access to it. We humans throughout time have come to believe many notions from this peripheral awareness, hense our mythologies and belief systems.

Janov suggested that our ability as humans to split off from traumatic pain and store it in the subconscious, is the way our species' survived, especially in childhood. It seems that no other creature has this faculty. There are several ways to describe it; we can call it "the split," or "repression" or the "subconscious." In any event it is an act of denial which continues until the traumatic experience is relived (fully felt), then the memory is restored to consciousness. Janov implied that the subconscious is only repressed pain.

7

The Defense System

Once a feeling has been relegated to the subconscious, Janov states, it remains there reverberating, seeking an outlet for expression. The feeling does not go away, although we have lost the memory of it (the connection).

When it finds a potential outlet, it starts to surface into consciousness, usually triggered when a similar feeling in the present occurs. It is at this point that we consciously begin to steer clear of upcoming feelings of pain. None of us like pain and instinctively will do our utmost to avoid it and make it go away. However, in this case we are steering clear of an already resident feeling, but are not fully aware of it.

As adults, we have many means of deflecting upcoming pain. In psychology these are called "defenses" or "act-outs." There is another called "act-ins, but I will talk about them later in chapter 16 on Medicine. Some of us take pain-killing drugs, nicotine and/or alcohol, others overeat or overindulge in other things like work, gambling or sex. It is our individual, deep-rooted means of defense that keeps us locked into neurosis for a lifetime. Psychology has suggested different act-outs (defenses) to be different diseases. Primal Theory implies they are just different manifestations (symptoms) of the same disease, namely neurosis.

The neurotic (subconsciously) is forever trying to resolve the hurt (trauma) of the past, by reproducing it in the present in order (hopefully and subconsciously) to resolve it. This never works, but the habit persists.

In Summary

Primal theory states that we as babies have needs which, if not fully met, cause us to suffer overwhelming pain which we then have to repress by splitting the memory of it from our consciousness. Unfortunately, this split from consciousness means we have no access through memory to this event, but are forever left floundering and only subliminally aware that something is amiss. Later in life, we develop defense mechanisms to prevent current feelings from recalling these deeper primal feelings which in turn permit the defenses to become embedded and reinforced as we get older.

Primal Theory suggests that nothing short of a reliving of the original feeling event will connect it back into our consciousness where the defense mechanisms will then cease to be effective or necessary.

Part II

The Implications

No one I know of has seriously challenged Primal Theory. I challenge anyone to do so. It has stood the test of the last 30 years and been validated by most working in this field. Because of this, I contend, there are implications.

Neurosis, as Janov defines it, gives us the means to defend ourselves from the initial (primal) pain. In childhood, that was necessary for survival, but as we grew older, and better able to survive, defenses act against us causing characteristics within us that we would really like to be without. The alternative is to relive the pain the defense system guards against. Alas, we instinctively run away from any and all pain. As a consequence, we become prisoners of this pain as Janov noted in his book *Prisoners of Pain*.

Until the discovery of Primal Pain and the underlying theory explaining it, we humans have been endeavoring to explain that "something in the back of our minds." Primal Theory identifies the problem and further implies that we humans are not that unique as creatures on the planet. Our uniqueness turns out to be a debilitating disease that we would be better without.

In part II of this book I will go into some of the implications to demonstrate this uniqueness as our problem and show several aspects of our way of life and our concepts of those features that I feel demonstrate all of this. Much of this will be contentious since allegorically, it "slaughters many sacred cows." I make no apology for this, but state it as simply and comprehensively as I can in the hope that my contentions make some ultimate sense and lend a sense of a reality we have never before contemplated.

8

The Mind

In a general way, we all know what the mind is and does, but specifically the mind is the physiology of the brain. By physiology we mean the workings of the brain. The workings of the brain contain many factors, not least of which are the automatic aspects of living like the heartbeat and the digestive processes and the instinctive reactions, but what I want to discus are the conscious and subconscious aspects of the mind.

The conscious mind

The conscious aspect is for the most part understandable insofar as we sense it. Some of the conscious aspects of the mind such as walking, working, talking and thinking seem normal, but how many of these latter ones are intrinsic to our being? Walking and working I suggest are, but talking is something that was developed at a much later time in our evolution. To demonstrate my point there is the story of a baby human left in the desert, picked up and raised by a gazelle. The child eventually learned to run and catch up with other gazelles, but it never learned to talk, which suggests that talking is not intrinsic. I understand there are other such examples.

The subconscious mind

I suggested in Chapter 6 what the subconscious was, but the subconscious is the most elusive part and we humans have been concerned about it for quite some eons by virtue of our lack of access to it. As I suggested earlier, this split away from the conscious mind creating the subconscious acted initially as a survival mechanism in our early childhood development, but later acted as a barrier to fully seeing ourselves in a total context and left us only with defensive mechanisms that we never fully understood. The child needed this facility; as adults we are left with this legacy hindering our ability to get the most out of life. Just knowing (being aware) of this aspect of the total mind might, I contend, be our greatest clue to unraveling many factors that religious, spiritual, cultural, philosophical and political thinkers have toyed with for centuries, never quite getting to the 'center of the cyclone' that we have been seeking.

The implications

I contend that all other creatures communicate with their own kind and perhaps generally with other species through the expression of their feelings. These expressions are most often sounds made vocally but can also be body movements and postures (including facial expressions). I contend that somewhere in our past we did exactly the same thing with grunts, groans, crying and laughing. This I feel preceded language as we now know it. Language is something we learn from others; we are not born with it. Consequently language is not intrinsic to our nature, but vocal expressions of our feelings were and are. It is our inability (because of neurosis) to fully express our feelings that has left us unaware of the very nature of feelings. In essence I contend that neurotics are only subliminally aware of some sensations—some of us more than others, depending on the level of repression in childhood.

Ways to envision the subconscious

Some ways to envision the subconscious might be: first, as a normal part of consciousness that splits away from the rest anatomically through the synapses (nerve endings in the brain). A great deal of work has been done in this area—mentioned at great length in Janov's many other books—that seems to be in accord with Janov's postulation. Second: as a blocking mechanism by us humans to deal with pain that was overwhelming to us as children. Third: as the part of the mind which subjectively denies that the feeling exists, in order not to feel it. In all cases, we sacrifice the ability to remember that event—we repress the memory. Hence it takes something as drastic as a reliving of the event to reconnect it back into consciousness or, put another way, to reconnect the synapses that created the split.

A thought about thoughts

Our human history, even those very vague aspects we see through archeology, takes us back no further than 20,000 years, but in terms of our history as Homo sapiens there were more than 80,000 years prior to that. What were we really like during that whole 80,000 year period? Our early writings, drawings, architecture and monuments only hint about the social life we humans lived by. It was obvious that we could do work and carry things, but at what point were we able to think?

Contemplate the concept

I ask you to contemplate this as a possible scenario without immediately attempting to dismiss it. If we can stretch to this point, then, I feel, most of the rest will fall into place. Most that read *The Primal Scream* seemed reluctant to accept the notion of hidden feelings. So, why did some get this and yet many others did not? My contention is it either touched on some deep feelings within us, or it didn't. If it did, we pursued further; if not, then it was merely just another idea.

Why my experience in that London clinic was important to me.

In my case, the London clinic incident stuck in my memory and, from time to time, I was acutely aware that I had had an experience that did not make total sense to me. I reasoned, in hindsight, that from the moment of being tranquilized, I did not complete the experience. I had many insights afterwards, but had I been allowed to complete the whole experience, I might have come to a similar conclusion as did Janov. Not that I would have been able to formulate Primal Theory, as I did not have the background to conceive this, but I know I would have known a deeper self. Others that I have met contend that *The Primal Scream* made great sense to them because, in almost all cases, it touched upon their subliminal feelings that there was something, demonstrating an unshakeable notion.

There is something unsatisfactory about life as we experience it now.

I can only appeal to the conscious mind and to the broader population's sense that there is something unsatisfactory by the way we are conducting life right now. I feel there is general dissatisfaction with the way most of us spend our lives. Where did all the joy and excitement go? I am not suggesting that life should always be pleasure, but when most of it, for most of us, is unpleasant, or at best just boring drudgery, surely there is something amiss. Why do so many of us now need to take antidepressants? There are many suggestions afloat as to how we might improve matters, but it is evident that most of these are band-aids and do not get to the core problem—said another way, do not get to the *Center of the Cyclone* as suggested by John C. Lilly in his book of that name.

Things are getting much too complicated like simply just doing and understanding the tax system. It appears we need a Ph.D. in rocket science just to program our mobile (cell) phones. Computers are not that simple or intuitive to use either and leave many of us frustrated much of the time. We get the same feeling in medicine and most of us refuse to even try and think in scientific terms. It's all rapidly becoming too complicated. I endeavor to rectify some of this by proffering Primal Theory as a new way to look at ourselves and the life we are involved in since, for the most part, the spiritual, political and rational modalities seem not to have given us any real overall answers.

At the back of our minds

If we are able to visualize that the conscious mind has a hidden component and that all it contains is stored pain, I feel that is all we need be aware of. We are not totally unaware of the subconscious, but merely think of it as *somewhere in the back of our minds*. Sadly, we jump upon any suggestion that proffers an explanation and we will believe many myths in order to reinforce our beliefs. Our known history of the human race (at best 10,000 years) is a testimony to just this. I will endeavor to look into some of these reckonings in the course of this book. We all know deep down there is something amiss. This something, I contend, has baffled us humans throughout our known history as evidenced by the mythologies which we still embrace to this day.

If thinking is done through language, as suggested by Benjamin Lee Whorf in *Language, Mind and Reality*, it might indicate that before language we did not think in the sense that we currently do. It is in this sense that we know animals do not think in the way that we think. Sure, animals use the left side of their brain to organize and express their feeling, but that is a far different matter than concocting mathematics. We initially merely reacted to feelings using the brain (mind) as do all other creatures on the planet. Thinking is a recently learned habit in terms of our evolution. The mind does way more things than just think and create ideas as I will attempt to elaborate in the next chapter.

9

The Nature of Thinking

thoughts, ideas and language

Thinking in language

If thinking is done through language as was suggested in the last chapter by Benjamin Lee Whorf, then the more we developed thoughts, the more we needed sophisticated language to formulate those thoughts.

Since language is something that evolved with us humans, then it would follow thinking too evolved in tandem with it, but what precipitated the development of language and hence thought?

I contend we started to think and use language at the onset of becoming neurotic. Unlike Freud, I do not believe that being neurotic is intrinsic to being human. There was a time in our evolution when we were not neurotic. If talking (the use of language) is an outcome of becoming neurotic, prior to that, I contend, we had no reason or need to talk. Make vocal sounds to express our feelings, yes. It was at the onset of neurosis that we humans talked in a vain attempt to express more clearly feelings many of which were now hidden in the subconscious—an extremely hard concept to accommodate.

Thinking is not intrinsic to our being

We humans have presumed that thinking is natural and normal to our species, but if we accept that as creatures we evolved, it is not hard to accept that there was a time when we did not think in the manner we now accept about thinking. Many meditation techniques are involved in eliminating the "ever-chattering mind." This suggests, to me, two things: first, that chattering and thinking are one and the same thing. Second, that there is a state of being beyond thinking. That state of being, I suggest, is simply feeling.

What is a full-feeling experience?

Janov stated that a full-feeling experience includes an expression component. That expression is processed in the thinking part of the mind. If all feelings have an emotional content and that emotional content is processed in the same area of the mind (brain) as thinking, then it is not too far a stretch to assume all thoughts are driven by feelings. If this is true, the implications are enormous and tell us a great deal about ourselves as creatures on this planet. The question here might be: what caused us to become neurotic in the first place? I will offer some propositions about this later in the book.

The development of language

However, as we became incrementally more neurotic, we needed a more sophisticated language to express our feelings. The notion that we think in language goes back at least to Benjamin Lee Whorf who in 1941, according to John B. Carroll in his book *Language, Thought and Reality*, suggested the link between language and thinking. He suggested that different languages involve a different thinking process, especially when comparing Indo-European languages with other languages. I contend that all thinking is done through language which suggests that abstract thought might not have been possible until we were able to record our speech (write). The nature of thinking has never been fundamentally studied to the best of my knowledge. We have merely accepted it *de facto* without questioning its nature or reasons for its origin.

If this thought process is done through language, as I have suggested, then thinking is not an independent action but is inevitably linked to feelings that, I contend, drive all thoughts. Hence before neurosis, we would have just felt and the mind would have processed that feeling with an appropriate mental process (emotion), in the thinking (left lobe) part of the brain.

Relegating feelings into the subconscious when they are overwhelming will separate them from the conscious process and I contend herein was the beginning of thought processes as we now know them. If this is true, then the implications are enormous and suggest, perhaps, there is little real difference between us humans and all other creatures—other than neurosis. It may turn out that we are not in fact the superior beings we have (through thinking) imagined.

The Evolution of thinking.

If we evolved as Charles Darwin suggested, then we did not always have language. Initially we merely uttered our emotions, like all other animals, through grunts, groans, laughter, crying, facial expression and body postures. Language was something we developed over time. I contend that language is not innate to humans. If we were not brought up and nurtured by other humans, would we have some form of language? I contend not. The story of the abandoned baby brought up with gazelles seems to corroborate this. Eventually, this human was captured many years later but could not speak or adapt to any form of humanness, least of all speech.

I suggest that all communication is only the conveyance of feelings. Hence we eventually developed language as we now know it as a sort of compensation for feelings we are not fully aware of. If this is a correct analysis of how we developed language, then Primal Theory implies that many of the utterances we began to make to convey feelings and intent became very symbolic. I contend that all language is symbolic and while it may appear initially to be more sophisticated, is nothing more than trying to express feelings.

All words in all languages, even the more primitive ones, are merely agreements among ourselves as to what we hope they mean. This agreement on what we are trying to convey is, as such, a very imprecise conveyance. One example: the language of law and science does its utmost to be precise, yet in both these fields ambiguity abounds. In particular, the phrasing of laws becomes more and more convoluted in order to be more precise, yet inevitably actually fails as evidenced in most courts of law around the world.

Language in its origins was very simple. It became ever more complicated and sophisticated as we grew increasingly neurotic. All we were trying to do, both initially and later, was to make our sentiments (feelings) known: communicate and to make sense, not to be intelligent. I contend that on a strictly living-creature level, there is only one thing to communicate: feelings.

The lazy-dog syndrome

I remember well my first lesson in classical geometry. The teacher walked into the classroom, looked at us all very sternly, then turned to the blackboard and began writing the following:

To prove: That a lazy dog equals a piece of foolscap.

Data: A piece of foolscap and a lazy dog.

Proof: A piece of foolscap = an ink-lined plane.

             An inclined plane = a slope up.

             A slow pup   = a lazy dog.

Therefore: A lazy dog   = a piece of foolscap.

                                         Q. E. D.

I contend this is the way most of us neurotics talk. We are able to make anything, through the use of words, mean anything we want or consider it to mean. My geometry teacher was aiming to convey the methodology of geometric proof by means of a parody. I see this syndrome used mostly by politicians—Karl Rove in particular—but scientists get caught up in it also. It is amazing how we will use a word in one context and then immediately use the very same word in another context and hope the original meaning carries over to the second instance hence, the lazy-dog syndrome. This trick works for the most part because we have become immune to the nuance of meaning and the ambiguity (in spite of dictionaries) of words.

Feelings and language

Feelings are communicated through the senses. We see another person, hear them, and perhaps touch them. Most of the time we sense from our own experience of feelings what is going on with the other person (often referred to as empathy). It is this empathetic nature that produces our greatest means of communicating and perceiving. Simply put, it is through our own feelings we tend to know what is happening to others. The most neurotic of us have the least empathy. Conversely, the most feeling-full of us have the most empathy.

I previously stated all we originally had to express were feelings. Initially, other than body movements, the only means were primitive vocalizations. It is not too far reaching to imagine that as we became a lot less feeling-full (neurotic), we needed to become decidedly more sophisticated to convey feelings (especially feelings that were already relegated to the subconscious). Initially, to convey what was happening to us, there were only nuances in the vocalizations. It would seem very natural that we would reach a stage of the early forms of language where we would indulge in vocal gymnastics. In other words, the less we had access to our feelings, the more we needed a sophisticated means of communication, hence the slow development of language, especially when misunderstandings arose because of our need to be more nuanced, so we used language as an attempt to convey what was going on as best we could. Since our deep subconscious feelings were inaccessible, we needed some very subtle means such as myth and rituals to explain them.

I also feel this would have been the beginning of what we now claim as our intelligence. The more feelings got relegated to the subconscious, the more ingenious we would need to become in order to explain and make sense of sensations going on deep within. This created the need to fathom explanations (myths) and those explanations that seemingly were the most acceptable to the community would gain general acceptance. It would then seem we had the division between the 'more clever' and the supposedly not-so-clever, or perhaps, the more divine and the less divine.

Ideas

The expression of ideas occurred more recently (in terms of the development of mankind). Abstract ideas came with the advent of writing (recorded speech): speech alone is way too ephemeral. We are now cluttered with just millions and millions of ideas with universities set up to disseminate them and, more recently, data banks to reference and maintain them.

Whatever else we say about words, they are only symbols—this book is full of them. It is the symbolism of words that gives us the greatest clue to their real significance. Once we begin to see that words are symbols, we might see more clearly that language is not some advanced manner of being, but just an advanced means of dealing with subliminal feelings or, said another way, a more nuanced neurosis. If we are not able to express feelings simply and clearly, then we need all the sophistication we can muster for the attempt. Our need to symbolize feelings through words gives us the means to see that language is an adjunct to, or consequence of neurosis.

Language, I contend, is only a highly-developed evolution of the gymnastics of the vocal chords and tongue, coupled with a highly-developed thinking structure as a way of compensating for a neurosis that hides most or many of our feelings. Looking at argument and debate, we begin to see why this method becomes ever more obscure and contentious and why its purpose almost seems to elude us. A look at any newspaper's letters to the editor demonstrates the absurdity of most arguments.

It is little wonder that we get lost in the wording of things. Perhaps the greatest example is in the use of words in our laws. The American Constitution is perhaps the greatest example of just this. We talk of intent and yet have little clue as what that intent (feeling) truly was. It got lost in its own definition. The Supreme Court deliberates on just this to a mind-boggling extent and what results is no more than the political wishes (desires) of the majority contestants (Supreme Court members).

Language that comes closest to the expression of feelings is that of poetry, novels and oratory. They are the most-admired forms of language. Language is the means we have to express our feelings and yet it is in this very sense we lose the ability to express them. We've assumed a fairness and unbiased deliberation form a supreme court, but their ruling in favor of George W. Bush in the 2000 election demonstrated their biases.

Psychology's use of words

Freudian psychoanalysis and Primal Therapy have taken advantage of the means to vocalize our feelings with words. Freud never saw the necessity to carry the process further towards the expression of those feelings, but rather left us with the notion that being aware was sufficient. For example, the slip of the tongue or the inadvertent mention of something that seemed to have nothing to do with the event in question. Primal Therapy aims to connect the use of words to the feelings behind those words. It also uses words to describe events and then moves us closer to the feelings involved in those events.

Thinking is not a higher state of mind.

If, as I contend, all thoughts are driven by feelings, whether old subconscious feelings or feelings in the conscious mind, then our ability to think is a direct necessity of our neurosis and not, as we have led ourselves to think, a higher brain function than any other creature. This I suggest is an "ego trip" on the part of humans, something I feel and fear we humans are going to be reluctant to accept. We have for far too long accepted the notion that our ability to think was some "higher state" of being. I am suggesting that we are inferior in our being than most other creatures because our thoughts are a function of our disease (neurosis). I suggest that we ought to give pause to our presumption of superiority over all other creatures. This might explain why we desire to control nature, unlike all other creatures, instead of embracing it. I contend our attempt to control nature will inevitably destroy it, us and the planet we depend upon.

The nine-dot syndrome

When I was about 14 years old, I read an article in the daily national newspaper about a Russian science professor recruiting scientists to work in nuclear physics. He set a problem for the applicants and if they were able to solve the problem within two minutes, he short-listed them. The problem was: There are nine dots (points) on a sheet of paper in the form of a square with three points equally spaced in three lines and all equally spaced from one another vertically and horizontally:

```
  .   .   .

  .   .   .

  .   .   .
```

He asked the applicants to intersect each dot (point) with four straight lines connected with one another consecutively so that the end of line one was the beginning of line two, and the end of line two was the beginning of line three, and the end of line three was the beginning of line four. I have posed this problem to many and only two people of over one hundred were able to solve it within the allocated 2 minutes. I, as a 14-year-old, was unable to resolve it even after several hours of trying.

If you are determined to try this, do it on a separate piece of paper before reading on.

The clue is: Open your boundaries.

The solution demonstrates just how we neurotics think. I will refer frequently in this book to what I call "the nine-dot syndrome," meaning that in most of our thinking we have boxed ourselves into preconceived notions, not stated initially.

Both the "lazy-dog syndrome" and "the nine-dot syndrome" demonstrate anomalies in our use of language. The most bogus for me is the use in general conversation of "positive" and "negative" regarding feelings, thoughts and/or attitudes. There is no general agreement out there (wherever out there is supposed to be) about what are positive or negative feelings, thoughts or attitudes (one man's positive is another man's negative; value judgment). I would prefer to use positive and/or negative only for battery terminals. If I wish to talk about feelings, thoughts or attitudes, I would rather use the phrase "I like" or "I don't like." This then becomes my feeling only and is not arguable. There is a tendency to use "right" and "wrong", "good" and "bad" also "polite" and "impolite" in the same manner. This I try to illustrate by using righteousness and/or wrongteousness. All these are value judgments. I will talk more about "values" in the chapter on economics.

Another factor of language I consider neurotic is to suggest some words are dirty or swear words. The word "fuck" comes to mind. I find this to be one of the most fascinating and expressive words in general use in the English language. One of the greatest arguments against its common use is that children ought not to hear or know it. I remember first hearing it at about age 5 and learning what it meant at age 8. Then, on going into government conscripted military service at 18, it became every other word for the drill sergeant. It was obviously sanctioned by the government and is now part of the language of "our brave military men." Sadly, I see nothing brave or noble about military men: they are merely professional killers and as such are amongst the most neurotic of us. I will talk about this later.

Ascribing attitudes and moralities to words is an absurdity and gets us into some of the most ridiculous debates and altercations amongst us humans. We begin to see our differences through these debates without realizing that all we are doing (deep down) is trying to express our subliminal (subconscious) feelings. I contend that our political affiliations and our ideas about everything we have opinions on are a very fundamental part of the pain in our subconscious. Said more clearly, opinions are created through our subconscious feeling, though we *reason* otherwise. We think we thought it all out—a myth. This is something Janov intimates about in his latest book *Primal Healing*. I contend that our languages are a fundamental part of our cultural heritages and will discuss culture in the next chapter.

10

Culture

Just as we understand the mind, we also have a general idea what culture means, but specifically our cultures are all those rites, rituals and beliefs that we have been brought up with. In my own culture, some of the rites and rituals are: so-called politeness, (asking others how they are when in fact we are not really interested), so-called decency (don't go naked in public), so-called honesty (don't take from others what is supposedly theirs) and so on. That we are supposed to be proud of our culture is a factor of culture. What exactly is there to be proud of? The rites and rituals over time have been seen to be barbaric in many cases. Is it possible that our current rites and rituals will also be seen to be barbaric in the future? In the past, the Western cultures have deemed it necessary to "civilize" other cultures when we in the West considered them barbaric by our standards. In more recent times, we have gone to the opposite extreme and looked at these cultures more benevolently.

Furthermore, our cultures also depend on what we believe in and that includes religion. Our religious (spiritual) beliefs are not intrinsic to our being. If they were, we would all believe in the same deity (or deities) and have the same set of moral values, but we don't. Besides, we would have always had these ideas throughout time, but we didn't.

I contend that all cultures are a factor of neurosis and vary according to geography, climate, childrearing, etc. Additionally, I feel culture, in general, is an inhibiting factor that maintains neurosis. Marvin Harris in his book *Cows, Pigs, Wars and Witches*, was asked why Hindus worshiped the cow. He studied this question, looked into similar questions in other cultures and concluded all cultures have their rites and rituals. These, he claimed, were a result of "mundane economic factors."

The mundane economic factors

Only when we study other cultures do we see the absurdity of many rites and rituals. Marvin Harris suggested in the case of the "sacred cow" that to slaughter the cow in order for starving people to eat would eventually have destroyed the whole culture and its people. The cow provided more nourishment over time from its milk and use of its dung as fuel for cooking. He suggested that the elders of the culture devised the sacred cow as a way to save the populace from wholesale extinction as a result of slaughtering their cows. Maybe those elders subliminally knew something, but the only way to effect compliance was by making the cow sacred.

First, no culture is static or monolithic. It revolves around what the current people of that culture arbitrarily on average agree upon. There are always dissenters. However, culture tends to be circular in nature by promoting itself and encouraging pride. Sadly, it is pride taken from an inferiority complex. The nature of rites and rituals within cultures (including my own) are way older than our modern and scientific notions that have now been proffered. But there is a very neurotic reasoning to perpetuate these rites, rituals and religious notions even when they are seen as counterproductive for that community. Neurotics are all hell-bent on keeping their rituals—rituals subliminally give a sense of the subconscious without actually explaining it.

It is here that the globalization of our Western culture and the advances in technology (started here in the West) seem to have gained the edge. Our exportation of this culture is being achieved through imperial colonization. We have assumed that our culture is the righteous one, hence our current desire to impose it. Alas, neurosis begets neurosis. The problem *is* the culture in and of itself.

It was only through the development in the West's studies of anthropology of other cultures and our conceited notion of superiority that we now may become aware of our own culture and how it inhibits us. When looking at culture through the lens of neurosis, we may better understand neurosis and culture and see the intertwining effects.

The imposition of our cultural, political, religious and philosophical ideas upon other peoples who initially had their own cultures was the most gross conceit and has, paradoxically, come back to haunt us now in what currently is being called the battle of civilizations. We are each terrified of the others' influence and the West, having the greatest influence and conceitedly believing in its own self-righteousness, is blinded to the others' attempts to defend their own. We are attempting to label their defending theirs as terrorism at worst, or primitive at best.

The quality of life can only be fully realized when culture is absent and we can be considered sovereign unto our individual selves and permit the demise of neurosis through more feeling-fullness.

Are there any non-neurotic cultures? Not that I know of, but there are some more neurotic than others and sadly, I contend, the Western culture and Judism are the most neurotic of all. Perhaps the indigenous peoples of the Americas and possibly some of the tribes of Central Africa, even Australia and New Zealand, might have been the least neurotic. This suggests there are quantitative aspects to neurosis. Because of this I feel we are able to make life-quality assertions about one culture over another.

Inherent in all cultures are the sexual mores of the culture. My next chapter will deal with sexuality and its impact in promoting the very neurosis we would like to transcend.

11

Sexuality

The nature of sex is two-fold: procreation and pleasure. Certainly we only indulge in sex with those we find sexually attractive unless we use sex to accomplish other means. The question here is: might we find someone sexually attractive and not be in love with them? I contend only sex addicts do this.

Ostensibly, we are born asexual, that is, without sexuality, or at least with a very primitive sexuality. I suggest that by age eighteen, both sexes are sexually mature, except for those that have been severely repressed. The "in-between time" is a process of going from no sexuality to a mature one. It is a process, not an instance of revelation as suggested by the notion of "just say no until marriage." I concede that there are moments in development when it might take on some acceleration, puberty being one. I feel that by deliberately denying children the natural process of sexual development and experimentation with themselves and their peers, we inhibit the learning process and then wonder why at puberty there are so many unwanted pregnancies and inhibitions about sexuality. I contend that if children were allowed to do their experimentations long before puberty (with relative safety from pregnancy), they would have adequate experience to prevent those pregnancies. Furthermore, I contend that a lot of the mysteries would be taken out of sex and also the cultural taboos, secrecy, shame, guilt and sinfulness.

I contend that children pick up, mainly from their parents, the no-no's of sex at a very early age, yet on reaching puberty (perhaps even before), know the thrill of sexual sensations—I certainly did. This sets off an incongruity in children and might account for much of their supposed difficulties and youthful rebellion. I further contend these no-no's of sex and sexuality do more damage than we have hitherto considered and implant in children's minds that there is something inherently wrong and/or dirty about sex. I feel that we tend to keep this attitude for the rest of our lives. Masters and Johnson commented on this.

One of the least-understood aspects of sex is the practice of using it as a painkiller and hence the current notion of sex addiction. This is my addiction—painkiller.

Normalcy

Sexual behavior is predicated on different patterns for most of us and includes all the exceptions we find amongst us humans. Some of these behaviors are classified as inversions and others as perversions. Inversion suggests unconscious deviating from the normal and perversion deliberately turning in the wrong direction. One's judgment as to whether a sexual act is inverted or perverted is a value judgment rather than a clear-cut definition.

This brings up the question: What is normal? If we are basing normalcy on average behavior, then we are duty-bound to get a 100% consensus as to what the limits are that most of us will respect in our lifetime. This is impossible; for the most part we assume that heterosexual sex is the norm and we do not deviate from traditional notions of that standard. Even Alfred Kinsey in his controversial study in the 1940s relied on what his interviewees were willing to admit to. Sadly, all through recorded time, we have assumed what is normal sex. Since most (if not all) of us are neurotic, it is not too far-fetched to understand that what is normal is more myth than fact. Even sadder is religious scriptures' reliance on this "myth" (as a standard template or guide) to promote their just punishments and admonitions. Saul of Tarsus, after leading a very suspiciously nefarious life, (according to one account, a murderer of Christians) had an epiphany on the road to Damascus and then preached for the rest of Christendom thereafter the righteousness of our sexual behavior for procreation only, based, presumably, on his own past experiences. His later beatification by a supposed non-sexual laity encouraged the rest of mankind to follow and observe.

Sex addiction

As I stated earlier, the use of sex as a painkiller is grossly misunderstood and only recently acknowledged as an addiction—using sex for something else, namely, a quick and easy thrill. I have personally fallen victim to this addiction. It took me many years before I was able to acknowledge that my sexual promiscuity was an addiction. It became for me a means of killing the subconscious pains that started to rise on an almost daily basis. For many years it was not obvious what I was doing. I just thought since sex was a natural act, my desire to indulge more often than most others was/is a factor of my sexual propensity. It was not until I paused acting out my sexual pursuits that I began to feel the rising pain behind it. It is our nature to attempt to resist pain which explains why and how sex has this addictive quality. The potential excitement aroused me and took me away from the rising old pains of childhood.

Manipulation

Using sex as a manipulative means is yet another diversion we neurotics use in our sexual activities. Prostitution is perhaps the most pronounced. It is my feeling that the most successful prostitutes (both male and female) are the ones whose sexual desires are not very important to them, money being perhaps their greater addiction. In this way, they see it as work and are willing to perform whatever service their clients seemingly desire. The nuanced types of prostitutes are numerous from the very polite and high class to the street hookers (hustlers) who deal in quantity rather than quality. However, there are many other ways to use sex manipulatively which occur even within romantic sexual relationships.

Children and Sexuality

If children were permitted to indulge in sex to the extent they desired, they would learn about sex in an orderly and natural manner with willing peers even before puberty. This learning would enable them to deal with puberty as it came along with a great deal of experience that would seem natural to them. Also, if from early childhood children were allowed to discuss their feelings, especially their sexual feelings, and they had a sense of trust with parents so it was not considered a "no-no," they would feel very free to discuss sex and be honest about what they did and what they felt. It would require that parents understand that it is vitally important that children have the freedom to ask and tell their parents whatever they need without retribution. It is assumed by neurotics that by not allowing discussion with their offspring that it will go away—another great myth as we each know from recollections of our own childhood.

Sexual deviances

All sexual desires are driven by pleasure seeking (including sadomasochism). That some desires to other people seem crazy stems from what each of us might consider "crazy." Some of these deviations I will mention here along with possible (not necessarily all) reasons for these deviant desires as a neurotic process.

Heterosexuality: the most common orientation between a male and a female, single or married. Within the framework of heterosexualality there are many varients.

Homosexuality: sexual indulgence between members of the same gender (either two males or two females) which may or may not involve some form of penetration. It is thought by many who have no desire to indulge in this sexuality that it is merely behavioral. Since I am homosexual, I have some experience in this matter. Although I do accept that at one stage in my history as a living creature I had a choice, it was a choice between life and death during my development as a fetus, not a sexual orientation choice. My sexual orientation could not be consciously decided as a fetus. However, making the choice to "live" constituted forgoing some natural development which meant that from there on I had no choice in the matter of sexuality (orientation). My sexual desires as I developed from as far back as I can remember were always about other males. This goes back in my case to age 4.

Bisexuality: indulgence with either sex. Most of the so-called bisexuals that I have known are usually choosing to indulge with one or the other sex based on some immediate convenience. These fall into two categories as I see it. The first is when a person is deprived of pursuance of members of the opposite sex in the moment. Since these people seem to have no inhibitions about sex with their same sex, then homosexual sex acts are not problematic for them. The second instance is where the preference might be the opposite sex, but because of other circumstances (military service, incarceration), it is easier to "get off" with a member of the same sex. These latter types are usually inclined to sex addiction, though not necessarily so.

Transsexuality: being born one sex and believing that one should have been born as the other is the most common reason offered for transsexuality and all its variants down to perhaps transvestites (cross dressing). I read recently on the internet the first chapter from a transsexual (Fierella) that made the transition, the hormone treatment and surgery to change the genitalia. She (born a male) warned all other transsexuals, and their varying nuanced others, of what is entailed in the transformation. She warned that it was not a pretty picture and led invariably to a not very satisfactory life. She insisted that her own reason to go through with this change was based on the prospect of having to live life as a male was far worse. It is my contention that perhaps in the womb or at least early in the very first year of life, one parent or the other did not want a boy (or girl as the case may be) and that the fetus or baby picked up on this and neurotically had no other recourse but to feel uncomfortable as the given sex. This then persists throughout life.

Pedophilia: (intergenerational sex): desiring sex with minors and sometimes prepubescent children. This is the most-hated sexuality in most societies, in one sense for very good reason—that sex with someone not at the same sexual development level causes the most profound disturbances in the younger (less-developed) member. Furthermore, sexual encounters between adults and children usually necessitate coercion of the child from the older person who often insists "this is not so." Of course, there are some examples where the younger person can be the instigator of the sexual encounter. Even so, the child is often coerced into going further than it really wants to go. I contend neurotics whose own sexual development was arrested at some earlier age will be tempted in their neurotic act-outs to return to sex with someone of that same age (symbolically) in order to resolve their own subconscious pain.

Beastiality: the desire to have sex with animals. I have met only two people that professed a desire to have sex with animals. Both worked on farms and both seemed to me to be very sexually repressed about sex with humans. I contend that their sex with animals developed because of their inability to be comfortable sexually with other humans. There are other examples of people being sexual with their pets perhaps for the very same reason.

Necrophilia: the desire to have sex with dead bodies. I have never met anyone that had this desire. However, I equally contend that this occurs with those that have an even greater problem than normal to express their sexuality with another human or with some living creature. It is a very severe neurosis.

Coprophilia: normally referred to as scat, indulging in sex involving defecation. I have never come across anyone indulging in this and feel that some connection in their childhood set some neurosis in motion that the participants in scatology are trying to resolve dating back to 'nappy' times.

Sadomasochism: taking sexual pleasure while being treated cruelly or wanting to treat the partner cruelly. I find it interesting that the few I have met that indulge in this, especially the masochists, feel the need, after punishment, to be loved and adored. I feel this is a direct connection with childhood punishment and a need for the masochist to resolve it. The child who only wanted love but all it got was punishment now acts out and takes the punishment only in order to be loved afterwards or punishes in order to alleviate the punishment doled out to them in childhood. This is a good example of recreating the past in the present in order to resolve it.

Root causes

All sexual deviations have their roots in childhood or even earlier in the womb. If this could be generally understood and accepted, it would help in childrearing and further prevent some of the damage that is inflicted on others in sexual encounters. We, as a species, need to reassess sex and our sexuality and know we are all different. Presuming we all are or should be the same is an indication of our own neurosis, hence in adulthood we act out in order to resolve our earlier conflict. Alas, all the acting out in the world never really succeeds in resolving the earlier childhood pain. Only fully reliving the event that initiated it will eventually allow resolution to begin.

One other factor of sex that underscores its furtive nature is our neurotic inability to talk about it openly and honestly. It is somehow always in the shadows demonstrated very clearly by parents at a loss for the most part to tell their children about it and especially how it created them. What are we ashamed of? I suggest that all of us neurotics are to some extent or other, deviant. To the Religious Right I say "let him that is without sin (deviance) cast the first stone." I contend that our sexual orientation is imprinted during uterine life or at the latest in the first year of life. Other factors after the first year may further reinforce the original proclivity.

Except for rape and attempts to coerce any other human (or creature) into a sexual act, or the deliberate willfulness to pass on a sexually-transmitted disease, having sex should be left solely to the people involved in the act. It is after all a private matter. Criminalizing some of these acts while allowing others, only further amplifies the neurosis within the community at large. If sex is a pleasure-seeking device, we should allow it provided all parties are willing and fully-informed participants. It is no more relevant than deciding what we want to eat or where we would like to go for a walk or whom we choose to have as friends. Feelings are the dominant factor.

Lastly, our understanding of sexuality does not derive from education, but rather from our experiences and our feelings and desires. My next chapter goes into the nature and meaning of education and how our current methods actually inhibit the very thing we are trying to achieve with it.

12

Education

All we need to learn is how to communicate and relate to one another and to perform certain tasks necessary to live with and within our community. Yet most of our formal education is about lots of extra stuff. The educational system places great value on this extraneous stuff. It is a paradox that the most sophisticated thing we ever learn, without being formally taught and long before we go to school or even pre-school, is to speak. Of course, it is only a rudimentary ability before we go to school, but considering the complexities of language, it is amazing that we learn it so early. We surely realize this when we try to learn our first foreign language in adulthood.

Schools, for the most part, are prisons for children and we expect the children to conform and learn in this very alien environment. This is crazy. Moreover, we have experts in the educational system who try to fathom what children should learn, at what moment in time (age) and by what method. Why is it not obvious we can let the child decide what and how and when it wants to learn anything, then go to the place (if allowed freely to do so) to get that learning? I say: Permit learning; stop teaching. This is the notion behind the "Free School" system first devised by A. S. Neill in England, in the early part of the last century, and written about in his book *Summerhill.*

A normal education teaches us nothing about life or living. Life is, in and of itself, a learning process. We neurotics tend to ignore this and instead presume we need to be educated about almost everything. We talk glibly about educating others about tolerance, about understanding of others, but these are not teachable subjects, mearly learnable, through feelings.

The bottom-up approach

What we need to learn is only what we desire to learn and only when we want to learn. If we understood Primal Theory, it might shed some light on this. Being taught is for the most part an imposition or coercion. If we were to leave it to the individual child (or anyone for that matter) allowing their own curiosity to lead to whatever they might find interesting and stimulating, I feel the child and society in general would benefit greatly. It should be obvious that one cannot force anyone into curiosity. Predictably, a child (and anyone else) is suspicious the moment we try to lead them there. What is needed is a bottom-up approach to learning. The top-down strategy is failing everwhere and yet we persist in it. Let each of us control our own destiny from the moment we are born. Children have a great deal to teach us—they are for the most part feeling-full. Might we be able to listen to them?

Don't we all remember the strictures of our days at school and isn't this the very problem we face currently without there seeming to be any solution?

Neurosis and the unlearning process

Neurosis is a learned behavior. We learn it very early when our options are practically nil. We have no real choice; the alternative would be death. Once we have learned to defend and act out in this manner, the only alternative (according to Janov) is to relive the pain of the original trauma. This, as I see it, is an unlearning process. It does occur somewhat naturally without seeming effort, but it is not that easy or that fast because we are forever running away from pain. If only we could sit down and face it—a mighty tough task I grant. Neurosis forces us into a behavior and inhibits, thereafter, our real nature.

If there is a need to be taught, then let's do it feeling-fully.

I contend that authorities will insist that teaching continues to exist. Nevertheless, a great deal of it could be accomplished feeling-fully. There are several exceptions to this and I will mention three:

1) Teaching people to kill, i.e. the military. By its nature, the only way to teach killing is to almost totally desensitize the student (soldier) first—madness.

2) Teaching prison wardens (guards) to keep incarcerated people in line to dole out punishment on someone else's behalf.

3) Dispatching police officers (so called "peace officers") to catch us, arrest us (restrain us) and then book us (humiliate us).

There are psychological consequences to teaching these professions and they are not pretty and cause damage to these professionals that are probably not felt till later in life.

If teaching is not done feeling-fully, then I contend it is not worth doing at all. This should be the criterion for any form of teaching or teaching instruction. If this were the prerequisite before instruction was considered, I feel we would see the necessity to eliminate a great deal of what we currently plan or hope to teach.

Montessori and other liberal methods

There is a presumption that children must be taught and hence the manipulative methods emanating from the Montessori mind-set. She assumed that first there was a necessity to teach (another of our tragic myths). Having made that assumption, she then attempted to teach in a friendlier manner. The fault with this system is the necessity to trick the student into learning (coercion), another example of "nine-dot syndrome." The school authorities and teachers in the Montessori system do have more control over what the students do and what they learn, but I feel that is no guarantee the student will learn. What we are left with is hope.

The free school system; creaed by A. S. Neill.

I mentioned Summerhill that A. S. Neill created and suggest reading his book of that same name if one is interested further. I will only mention here that Neill, a Scotsman, was inspired by a probation officer who asked his probationers how best they could assimilate back into society and be helped to do this. It was inspiring to him that many of them had numerous original ideas on the matter. Neill, accepting that premise, thought it applied equally to his own profession, teaching, and set out to experiment and to demonstrate his findings. An intriguing read for the open minded.

It seemed when I was young and in school that education for the most part had sorted itself out and that was a peaceful and a relatively easy passage for children. By the next generation, there were some problems arising and many suggestions as to how to rectify most of them. Some were political, others authoritarian. The authoritarians seemed to have won the battle but then as time has passed, the problems have worsened till now it seems they are insurmountable. Why is this? I feel that our current path of believing in a top-down system of governance on all levels—business, institutions, even churches and education—is showing that we took the wrong path. I contend that until and unless we reverse this trend in practically all walks of life, we are doomed to destroy ourselves and the planet.

Neurosis begets neurosis

One of the factors of neurosis is that the more neurotic we get, the more neurotic we make the next generation. Neurosis has the habit of replicating itself. Much like alcoholics, until we can begin to accept the notion that we are neurotic, we will fail to eradicate it. Like alcoholics we need to accept the situation as a disease and then study the means to combat it. The prerequisite for joining Alcoholics Anonymous is to admit that one is an alcoholic. Failure to do so compounds the problem. There is a need to understand first that we are neurotic; only then might we seek to get beyond neurosis or better still prevent it in the first place. Nicotine addiction is now falling into the same category; finally there is this notion amongst youth that it is no longer "cool" to smoke; an addiction that causes a great many problems, not only for smokers themselves, but also the population at large. The only people still in denial are the tobacco growers and manufacturers who, driven by profit, will concoct any illusion of legitimacy.

The education lottery

The idea that education is for sale is perhaps the greatest argument against the current system. Until money and privilege are eliminated, it will remain corrupt and we will see people becoming professionals in work that is unsuitable for them or their employers. It is generally understood now in America that if you buy your education well, you will gain a more lucrative living. If this is true, it goes counter to all the educational testing that has ever been created. The current system is broken, corrupt and inefficient. It has become a system for the highest bidder. George W. Bush is a case in point: the class dunce that made it to the presidency because mommy and daddy were able to buy it. Paradoxically, he, Bush, promotes meritocracy!

Time spent away from the learning process

It is important that time spent away from the learning process is as important as the time spent in it—in order to absorb it. I learned this lesson from working in the English theater system of "weekly rep." You learned a play in one week while you performed another in the evenings that same week. Universities are bordering on the same intensive learning approach. It actually goes against the very learning process we hope to achieve. Then, at the end of the course, what the student starts to do as a living is often remote form the very nature of the studies involved. Crash courses fall into the same category and usually finish up being counterproductive.

Here in the United States, higher educational facilities rely on sport to make much of the revenue to stay in business. This is gross capitalism out of whack and even worse, the coaches of these sports are often paid many times the amount of the highest-paid deans. Is there something wrong here? It is an incongruity that sport is used to finance higher education. The two topics are unrelated but seemingly this practice has been allowed to transpire especially here in the United States. I discuss sport is my next chapter.

13

Sport

The thrill of winning

Sport is competition; the ultimate competition is war. The neurotic makes life competitive. "Me or You." A fully-feeling person would want life to be cooperative—"Me and You." There are two aspects of sport: the first as participant, the second as spectator; in either case it is an outlet for anger called entertainment. Participating is considered healthy physically, but it has a detrimental effect psychologically because it is stressful to compete. The neurotic's desire to indulge in and/or watch sport ameliorates the anger within us. Alas, it is symbolic anger and will never be resolved until we are willing to face and relive the original anger now locked into the subconscious. Sport in this sense is a major neurotic act-out.

I contend that violence is an attribute of a lifetime of pent-up anger in ones subconscious. We talk glibly these days about anger management, but I contend that we will never eradicate violence (bottled up anger) in an individual until we can deal with the underlying anger in that person's subconscious: anger that originated there for a very good reason in childhood.

Machismo (being manly)

The so-called physical attribute of sport is only for those people who are tough, strong and athletic. This sets male children up to aspire to be tough and strong instead of encouraging feeling-fullness, gentleness and caring. Girls are not so bombarded, although 'tomboys' often will aspire in a similar manner. For the most part, females are encouraged to be more sensative.

Competition is healthy—a myth. We are not naturally competitive, guarded or defensive until we are threatened and this is seen clearly in most other creatures. That we may consider ourselves different is one of the reasons I feel that we have assumed competition to be healthy. The health issue is something I will talk about in the chapter on medicine. Is there a real necessity for the body to overindulge in that amount of exercise? I contend not. That amount of physical exertion is only possible in the earlier part of adulthood leaving the athlete in limbo both emotionally and physically after midlife. Furthermore, we now see the number of ex-athletes suffering from this over-indulgence of the body and how it wrecks the body later in life.

Spectator sport is complicated psychologically causing many psychological ramifications both by winning and worse by losing. It offers admiration if your side wins and a camaraderie that is more often fake than real. Then there is a weird sort of gloating over the opposition. Being the spectator to sport lets the other guy risk body and limb.

The thrill factor

In a neurotic world where there is very little to stimulate us emotionally, we are up for grabs for anything that might stimulate. The roar of a crowded sports stadium is like a mass hysteria which is ostensibly allowable with grown men falling back on a childhood glee.

It's always a win-lose factor. Someone always loses and when a team starts to get into a losing streak, there is the tendency to disassociate from the loser. This is a very serious lack of compassion which often can only sustain itself if the team is local and one associates very closely with the locale. It's another way of dividing us from one another. It is a major counter-cooperative social act.

It might be considered beneficial socially if it does ameliorate anger. This is at best a *band-aid* and serves to put everyone in denial about what is really taking place. We are merely keeping the "lid on anger" to an acceptable social level. We are forever adjusting the rules to keep the anger under 'wraps'. There is a very real need socially to get to some fundamental causes at the root of a lot of our anger. We endeavor to maintain control with more sophisticated repression, but resolve nothing in the final analysis.

Sport used as a means to finance education should be cause for concern, especially in view of the saleries paid to these coaches. Surely a contradiction of what the education system is really all about.

Children naturally play and what they mainly play is sport-type games. This is another myth since child's play often attempts to imitate what they see adults around them do before they get into sport play and competitiveness.

Means to fame

For many kids in the ghetto, their only means to see a way out is aspiring to fame and riches through sport. This is a pathetic scramble for those kids and causes some of the most serious psychological problems for the majority who inevitably fail. Could gang membership be one of only a few ways out of this dilemma for youth and especially the deprived and poor?

Drugs and sport

For the desperate and those that nearly make it, drugs are the mecca/savior; sporting authorities see this as cheating to win. To the sportsperson it may often be his/her only chance at success (if only he/she can get away with it).

If sport is stimulation of some feelings, then art is an even greater range of emotional stimulants and the subject of my next chapter.

14

Art

Art is the artificial stimulation of feelings.

It is the stimulation that is artificial, not the feelings. If the stimulation were not artificial, it would be real life. The feelings must be real; otherwise we would never be moved by them. The artist (creator) is inspired by feelings which are expressed through the medium of their choice. The purpose of art in a neurotic world is to stimulate some feelings within the spectators/audience through the artist's medium. The artist is also operating from their feelings which beget further feelings.

It is little wonder that music is very predominant in our neurotic world because, in our early evolution, we used sound almost continually to convey feelings. I contend we are somewhat instinctively attempting to return to our primal nature with the use of music.

Purpose

The purpose of defining art is to mark the boundaries of what it encompasses. To the best of my knowledge, no one has ever defined it. Art, like many other things, is something we subliminally recognize but can never be clear about. In defining it, I consider that we may more clearly see why we humans create and use it. In a neurotic world, we need all the emotional stimulation we can get. Art also gives us a greater chance to channel our feelings and emotions. We get a sense of being in control. I contend this is another misunderstanding we humans have about feelings. We are only able to control the emotions (responses) to feelings, but Primal Theory demonstrates that there is no way we can control our actual feelings. Feelings happen "willy-nilly"—whether we like it or not—at all times, resulting from what is happening all around us. Art, in this respect then, may be a social necessity to sublimate some of the more primal feelings lying dormant and attempting to seek expression. In this respect, sport too could be considered a social mediator of the expression of our feelings, but with a lesser range of feelings.

However successfully we are able to repress our feelings, I contend we are never able to fully achieve it and perhaps the closest we ever come is with catatonic patients. Total non-feeling occurs only at death. Janov suggested that neurosis is working at all times (even in sleep) and never lets up. If this is true, and I feel it is, it is a sorry state of affairs for us as a species.

It may be postulated that perhaps we could use art to promote a more feeling-full world. I contend, however, the reverse is true and having some outlet for our feelings and a limited (emotional) response actually feeds into our neurosis and encourages us to maintain the status quo. So, far from it being a noble pursuit, I see it as an inhibiting factor to reliving those deep, early feelings and bring them into consciousness. In a non-neurotic (fully-feeling) world, art would become redundant. I further contend that is why no other creatures attempt to artificially stimulate feelings. They just simply accept what exists in a feeling-full way and respond appropriately.

Demystifying art

By demystifying art, I feel we are in a better position to see how we might attempt to create a life, especially in the rearing of our children, that is more feeling-full. This would not be a quick or easy process, unless there is some consensus by the population as a whole. Since not all feelings are pleasant. A feeling-full world would not, by definition, be utopian (what ever is deemed utopia). However, since feelings are the one thing we have little or no control over, I feel there would be a greater acceptance of those feelings that we did not like (normally referred to as negative) and more direct ways to prevent the unlikable feelings from reoccurring unnecessarily. I feel the very nature of life and living (the so-called purpose) would provide a natural and simple understanding from childhood onwards. Life is merely about experiencing what is happening to us from moment to moment. In the final analysis, life would be a sum total of the billions and billions of moments like now—"now" having moved on to another "now."

I contend that an understanding of Primal Theory would help us see more clearly many of the problems we humans face in our general traversal of life. I don't feel it will necessarily eliminate any of our current problems, but it might give us some insight as to how to look at life and some of the problems we are forever trying to resolve. By defining art, we do not take away any of its magic. The real magic is contained within the feelings. Referring to this magic as being mysterious merely suggests that we were never able to explain it. I feel Primal Theory will take the mystery out of our thinking, but in so doing will add to the magic.

It has been our attempt to demystify things that led us down the path trying to fathom the whys and wherefores, which brings me to my next chapter on science.

15

Science

trying to explain the inexplicable

Science is our attempt to understand ourselves and our environment. It's been a grotesque failure insofar as we are no nearer to understanding ourselves or the environment. Science is premised on the word "why" and, as far as I know, exists in all languages. We are the only creatures on the planet wanting to know why and having a desire to know. The paradox: the more we understand, the less we know we understand. The question "why" never gets fundamentally answered. For example, if we pick up a stone and drop it and then ask a child, "Why did the stone fall?" the child might simply reply, "Because you let go of it." Later, the child in high school is doing elementary science and the teacher asks the student, "Why did the stone fall?" and the student now replies, "Because the air underneath the stone is less dense than the stone." When that student becomes a senior and the teacher asks, "Why did the stone fall?" the student replies, "Because of the acceleration due to gravity." Later we might ask, "Why gravity?" Physicists are still battling this one out. I contend that the reason we humans ponder this is because we subliminally understand that we are not fully connected to the mind which is estranged from subconscious feelings, yet we make an attempt to explain what is in essence, inexplicable.

The body of science is testament to the neurotic nature of science itself. The bickering, backbiting and egocentricity within the scientific body are concomitant with the nature of the pursuit, contrary to what has been perceived as a noble profession. We seem incapable of getting to the core of our problems because we assume, what in effect, was never stated—the nine dot syndrome. An example: the search for an ideal passenger transport vehicle without ever asking the real fundamental questions in the first place. Hence we finish up with a two-human-wide automobile when 95% of the time there is only one person in it, adding to the space it takes in roadways, parking facilities and garages to accommodate it. Yet we do nothing to rectify this with a narrower automobile as our roadways and parking facilities become more and more congested. Better yet, a single-wide automobile need be one-tenth the weight of the average four-seater we now run around in, be less dangerous and could easily cut down on the energy needed to propel it. The automobile is too wide, too heavy, too dangerous, too complicated, too polluting, too conjesting, too expensive, and yet we do little about it.

The nature of why

What *is* science is encapsulated in that one word "why". Science, as I see it, is our attempt to better understand and serve ourselves, our environment and our lives. Have we actually achieved this? I feel we have not in any real sense. I feel we fool ourselves into thinking we might. Again: the more we think we understand, the less we know we actually understand, yet we stay in this merry-go-round ever seeking more answers. I feel if we were cognizant of Primal Theory, we would be in a better position to see what we are actually trying to achieve. "Understanding," it was once said, "is the booby prize." Deep feelings are the royal road to being fully integrated—creating real understanding. Knowing this, might it be possible to abandon many of our scientific pursuits?

It is interesting that all the above explanations for the stone falling are valid; however, each explanation begs the next one. Just how far do we need to go in the world of explanations and does it help us live a better quality of life? Primal Theory intimates that explanations resolve nothing.

The reason we humans have this particular kind of curiosity is because deep down we subliminally understand that we are not fully connected to ourselves and we have a split that divides our conscious from the subconscious. The organism is forever attempting to reconnect, even though we are not conscious of that effort. Our notion that we are more inquisitive creatures turns out not to be the noble trait we've presumed. An example of our thinking is the "nine-dot" syndrome. We presume boundaries and conditions that are not stated or explicit, hence we cannot accept the notion (much of it legacy) of a single-person-wide automobile

We've also claimed that our search for knowledge has caused us to discover and invent some very convenient ways to make life more comfortable, but in view of more recent understandings about our environment, we have not, in effect, made life easier or even more pleasant. We have indeed created some of the most devastating contraptions that actually now threaten our existence, nuclear bombs being our maddest. But even other inventions that seemed so benign now threaten our ability to live comfortably on the planet. The internal combustion engine comes readily to mind, creating millions of road deaths and perhaps "global warming" that might actually destroy our climate and threaten survivability.

Using our minds—disconnected from feelings behind the thoughts—we search to understand these thoughts, but fail to accomplish real understanding—a paradox. Were we to connect the feelings behind the thoughts, I contend, we'd know real understanding and see the irrelevance of 95% of our searches.

We devise complex problems in order to come up with simple solutions. We have it backwards. If we were to devise simple problems, we might find better solutions. The result could be extremely complex, but the alternative leaves us without real solutions. I contend we ask complex questions because we often presume a solution beforehand—the very hallmark of neurosis.

Scientific progress has not improved the quality of life; we've merely presumed that life now is better than it was. The real quality of life encompasses the quality and depth of our feelings and our ability to appropriately respond to those feelings. This is a hard concept for most neurotics to comprehend.

The obvious question most asked is: Do we want to go back to the Stone Age? My response is, No! We need to go back (or forward) to the Feeling Age which, incidentally, is further back than the Stone Age. Paradoxically, the Stone Age set us on the pursuit of science. The only way to make life more bearable is to first begin to be feeling-full within it. The rest will follow naturally.

Stephen Hawking, one of the great scientific minds of the present, in his book *A Brief History of Time*, sets out to explain warped time and demonstrate string theory. The explanation asks that we accept up to 11 dimensions. How does one get one's mind around more than 4 dimensions? Even 4 boggle the mind for many of us. The only way to conceive it is taking the one dimension, time, and stating that it, in-and-of-itself, has three dimensions, hence the construct of warped time. In order to perform this mental gymnastic we first need to eliminate our instinctive notion of time as linear—almost as absurd as the notion that the earth rests on the back of an infinite tower of turtles. The first paragraph of *A Brief History of Time* starts:

"A well-known scientist (some say it was Bertrand Russell) once gave a public lecture on astronomy. He described how the earth orbits around the sun and how the sun in turn orbits around the center of a vast collection of stars called our galaxy. At the end of the lecture, a little old lady at the back of the room got up and said, 'What you have told us is rubbish. The world is really a flat plate supported on the back of a giant tortoise.' The scientist gave a superior smile before replying, 'What is the tortoise standing on?' 'You're very clever, young man, very clever,' said the old lady, 'but it's turtles all the way down!'

Most people would find the picture of our universe as an infinite tower of turtles rather ridiculous, but why do we think we know better"

Indeed why do we think we know better? The answer lies in our *thinking*. In his conclusion to *A Brief History of Time,* Hawking states:

"We find ourselves in a bewildering world. We want to make sense of what we see around us and ask, what is the nature of the universe, what is our place in it and where did it and we come from?"

Why is it the way it is?

I suggest it is the questions that are absurd and result from our neurosis. I contend that if we were not neurotic, we would have no need to ask the questions in the first place, but would be content to feel what is happening around us and respond to those feelings appropriately. In this sense, science and our scientific curiosity are just another neurotic act-out for killing pain, no better, no worse, than any other act-out, but an "act-out" nevertheless.

Biological evolution is not a matter of trial and error, but functions by using its feelings to progress to the next step. As we feel, so do all other forms of life. The feelings of other forms of life are a tool towards their survival, not chance and not understanding.

Behavioral studies are irrelevant and teach little or nothing. Experimentation on animals (a neurotic pursuit if ever there was one) like dissecting frogs is school butchery called biology. Why not study the biology of other creatures as feeling-full beings and see if this could not equally be applied to our own species? It is the nature of life as well as death. Cause and effect appears in the feeling-full parameter, the cellular permutation. Are there feelings on the cellular level? Primal Theory intimates that is so.

Real knowing

The only thing we truly know is what we feel. All other so-called knowledge is irrelevant; circumstantial evidence at best. Why do we think one way or another? Things are only the way we feel (perceive) them. We have given science an accolade it does not deserve. We first assume that scientific development is the only natural course of events. Growing older is a development. We all instinctively understand development on that level. However, when we take the two meanings of development and combine them into one, we assume that scientific development is the same as any other use of that word—the "lazy-dog" syndrome. Science and scientific development have only begun to expand in more recent times. This curiosity quest gives us the "raison d'être" for science. Science and the curiosity quest were meant to make things easier for us, but have we indeed benefited from science? Certainly the development of the nuclear bomb is very questionable.

Curiosity, seen as good, normal, or natural, is a myth; there is nothing eminent about scientists who squabble like cats and dogs and are as egotistical (neurotic) as the rest of us.

The search for the ultimate formula

Our search for Unified Field Theory is ongoing, but I contend that by 1970 Unified Field Theory had been found. Sadly, it was not recognized and perhaps still isn't. However, Unified Field Theory, I say, turns out not to be in science, physics or technology. Unified Field Theory turns up, of all places, in psychology. I feel that Primal Theory *is* Unified Field Theory. My reasoning is because the nature of thinking has never been questioned by the scientific community. In this context, Hawking's flat earth, lady's "tower of turtles" thinking was no less plausible than "string" or more recently "membrane" theory. How, unless we have blind faith in mathematics—just another agreed upon language—do we picture this concept?

Albert Einstein's development of "The Theory of Relativity" coincidentally used the word "relativity." Anything is arguable, and perhaps reasonable, depending upon what it is relative to. If time is multi-dimensional, are we not mentally attempting to disappear up our own assholes (figuratively speaking)? Is this 'thinking' carried to some neurotic extreme? I feel his use of "relativity" was no accident.

Devising Unified Field Theory and the search for it are seemingly science's greatest goal. We've been searching the mind for this once-and-for-all explanation, but the real question is why *do* we pursue it? It's a neurotic pursuit. Once we understand the madness of the pursuit and then know why we attempted it, will we be able to rectify the sickness (neurosis) rather than acting it out using science.

We fail to grasp the total use of the mind to delve into and understand the world around us and also fail to see that the use of the neurotic mind to make the search is exactly where the problem lies. It is this manner of using the mind that ought to beg the question: "Why are we pursuing this?" Herein lays the reason that Unified Field Theory turns up in psychology and not in physics.

Computers and their place in society provide just another toy. In primal terms, the scientific quest is nothing more than neurotic hope that we are going to resolve our problems as a species. It is my contention that a feeling-full community would not have a curiosity drive unless that desire was to resolve some simple local community problem like how to get the water out of the well. We have long since accepted too many myths surrounding science and as such given it license it should never have had. It is little wonder that we are intent on creating machines that can run us, decide for us, analyze us and to some extent control us. Is this not the essence of madness, better known as neurosis?

Most so-called scientific research these days is statistical evidence. If this process of averages is meant to be science, then we are in even deeper trouble. Statistics can seemingly be manipulated in so many ways that we find most "studies" coming to conclusions that the studies hoped and planned for in the first place. Where did we hear this before? We hear what we wanted to hear, not necessarily what was actually said—the "nine-dot" syndrome. The final decision to be made by ordinary people is to stop permitting scientists to tell us how we ought to be, but rather let each of us decide for ourselves (from within our feelings). Let's put the scientists back in their *box* and say "Get on with your doodling with two provisos. First: do no harm to anyone or any creature. Second: do it at your own expense, not ours."

16

Medicine

trying to cure the incurable

As an adjunct to science, we have medicine which I feel has set us out on a path of searching for cures. We seemingly fail to research prevention, supposedly because prevention will hardly bring in revenue (profit). However, in the pursuit of cures, we have relied heavily on pharmacology to come up with answers. My feeling is that pharmacology creates as many problems (side effects) as it seemingly eliminates. Also, medicine, in its researches, attempts to seek solutions through microbiology. We've lost the wholeness. We are becoming so sophisticated in this pursuit we are losing sight of what we surely hoped to achieve: a decent quality of life.

It is amazing that we still do not understand the nature of addiction. We can only get addicted to substances and behaviors that kill pain. The proclivity to become addicted is not a genetic, hereditary or chemical-dependency factor. These notions are examples of looking through *the wrong end of the telescope,* or nine-dot syndrome. The simple notion that we naturally will do our utmost to avoid pain (even in light of knowing that killing the pain ultimately is killing us) explains it all. Nothing further needs to be understood. "Why did the stone fall?" "Cause you let go of it," the child said.

I feel if the medical profession were first to look at and then study Primal Theory, they might find many answers to both prevention and ultimately the eradication of many of those strange diseases like cancer, heart disease, depression, Parkinson's, Alzheimer's, Hodgkin's, etc. which I feel are the ultimate results of a lifetime of reverberating feelings in the subconscious (neurosis). They are not accidents nor are they pure misfortunes. They are our deep, unfelt feelings having spent decades looking for resolution and the freedom to express them. The disease becomes an "act-in," yet another means of defending against upcoming pain. I suggest that there is only one fundamental dis-ease (ill at ease) and that is "neurosis"; all other diseases are a symptom of that one malady.

Prevention/cure anomaly

Medicine has forever been concerned about curing, taking little notice of prevention. I would like to suggest that Primal Theory shows the way to prevention. I do grant however that Primal Therapy is an attempt to cure the damaged neurotic. If, as I have claimed, the discovery of Primal Pain is the greatest discovery mankind ever made, then I feel the promulgation of Primal Theory could bring about our greatest effort to prevent most of these so-called diseases of old age and many others.

Medicine is only a specialized extension of science and as such falls into many of the problems I laid out in science. However, because it involves our being, it has a greater impact upon us. Our ignorance of why we get ill suggests there is some disconnect here. That is the same disconnect we have with the conscious/subconscious split. It is for this reason that I feel we neurotics found ourselves only able to look at symptoms and then see if we could resolve them—the "nine-dot" syndrome—historically, first by potions and voodoo, later via chemicals and now pharmaceuticals. The only other methods have been through surgery (barbers and bloodletting), then on to amputation of the offending part or organ. Now we've progressed to a point where we either try to reproduce what we have surgically removed or, even better still, replace it with someone else's body part (dead or alive); also now we're trying to grow it from parts of our own body through what we hope we know about DNA (stem-cell research). Alas, all this still attempts to *close the barn door after the horse has bolted.*

As we progress into deeper understanding of microbiology, we look for the mysteries and, as in science, generally find more questions than any real solutions.

One other area that medicine has labeled a medical problem is obstetrics. Every birth is considered a medical problem/concern and provides an example of something that was once the very essence of being female. I contend that the interference of the medical profession into this area has progressively created a self-fulfilling prophecy. It now has become almost impossible to avoid medical intervention for the birthing process. However, I contend that very intervention has actually exacerbated the difficulties successive generations of child-bearing women have encountered. Furthermore, medical interventions are exacerbating the very neurosis (trauma) that I have hitherto written about, demonstrated by Dr. Frederick LeBoyer in *Birth Without Violence*. I will discuss more on his findings in the final chapter on childrearing.

The latest mad craze to produce organs and replace the ones we've ruined and abused is but a short step to cultivating humans solely for the purpose of organ availability for those of privilege who've abused and destroyed their own. I personally would not rely on ethics or ethicists to resolve this for us as I will further explain in the chapter on religion.

Drugs and their use

The dictionary defines drugs as any medication. It is not medication I want to discuss, but what are often referred to as narcotics or mood-enhancing substances. There are three types of drugs in this category: the ones prescribed by doctors, those sold over-the-counter (which include tobacco and alcohol) and the others that are deemed illegal.

Type 1) The legally-prescribed drugs. Many of these are mood elevators in the form of stimulants and antidepressants. The psychological effects of these substances are just as problematic as the illegal mood elevators, but being prescribed and dispensed in pharmacies gives them legitimacy.

Type 2) The legal non-prescription mood elevators. Here in the West they are mainly tobacco and alcohol although there are some milder ones like valium and aspirin and other over-the-counter (non-prescription) drugs.

Type 3) The illegal drugs. These consist almost exclusively of mood elevators—pain killers—and are most commonly heroin (the king of painkillers), cocaine, methamphetamines and ecstasy.

Almost all of the above types are painkillers except for some of the stimulants. Three illegal drugs, the opposite of pain killers, are marijuana, lysergic acid (known as LSD) and peyote (a mushroom), but as feeling enhancers are not really addictive in the real sense but enjoyable, especially if they don't encourage unpleasant feelings, which they can.

Addiction

The medical profession has never really come to terms with the nature and definition of addiction. I contend that Primal Theory lends itself to demonstrate exactly what addictiveness is. I repeat, one can only become addicted to painkillers. There are no genes or character tendencies for addiction. Someone in pain will seek (naturally) to alleviate it. This implies that anything that kills or ameliorates pain can become addictive, be it a substance or a behavior. Once it is understood by the healthcare profession and legislators that addicts are individuals with rising pain, then there is a chance to see a way beyond it. The problem for neurotics is subconscious pain. Alleviating the root cause of this pain is tricky. Medicating the pain (killing it) is one possibility, but always a never-ending process, hence causing addiction. The only alternative is reliving the pain—Primal Therapy. However, that is a much more long-term process and, without help, almost impossible. Invariably, what happens is the addict substitute's one act-out for another, usually more socially-acceptable one, but often no healthier in the long term. The 12-step programs are examples of just this. Not that these programs do not offer some temporary relief—they do—then we become addicted to the program.

The healthcare industry and the healthcare systems are, for the most part, concerned with making maladies and afflictions, bearable. Afflictions most often precipitated by reverberating (subconscious) old pain. If this could be understood by healthcare professionals, I contend we would be able to see better ways to treat these maladies and, better still, ways to prevent them. See Janov (1996) *Why You Get Sick-How You Get Well.*

Depression

Though depression might concievably come under the heading of psychology; my next chapter, I will touch on it here. Depression is the most acute example of feelings rising up from the subconscious. Anyone suffering this malady, which includes many of us, will know the excrusciating pain held in the subconscious and see clearly why we do not want to feel it. Alas, all the medical profession is able to do is to medicate us out of it, but like all medications of this nature, is never ending. There have been some suggestions amongst the psychiatric profession to postulate that it might even be a virus. This, I contend, is a gross neurotic speculation. Janov suggests that it is almost impossible to eradicate deep depression without plunging into the depths of the unconscious (subconscious) where the basis of it all lies.

17

Psychology

(why we think and behave the way we do)

The implications of Primal Theory are enormous and prompted me to write this book. At first, I needed to decide whether Primal theory is valid. A theory is a model through which we are able to look at some phenomenon and make sense of it. The notion "the exception proves the rule" is utterly illogical. A theory whereby all of the observable factors seem to fit in to the current parameters is valid. I am convinced that Primal Theory is valid.

Too often, scientific investigators try hard to squeeze a theoretical framework to fit their preconceived ideas—the lazy-dog syndrome. This, I contend, is neurosis at play in what Freud coined the "ego." I suggest that the "ego" is what we *hope* others think about us, while we know deep down that is not who we really are—hope springs eternal.

In the case of Primal Theory, Janov's observations had taken place prior to his delineations. After he observed the reliving by his patients, he listened ever more carefully to the tapes of the sessions he had made of the first two patients. As he stated,

> "Slowly some meaning began to emerge. … Theory, I
> must emphasize, did not precede clinical experience."

It was the integrity of Janov that gave great credence to his findings and that led to the book becoming a best-seller. However, when Janov was reluctant to allow psychologists to practice from merely reading his book, many professionals started to question it mainly on the basis of its simplicity, assuming that something so simple could not be valid. We (not the professionals) need to reconsider this after 30 years of neglect.

No real profound psychological theory has been proposed since Primal Theory. There have been many who have elaborated on current notions of psychology by just tweaking some prior idea. Most of these theorists base their success on the efficacy of statistical subjective responses from patients and for the most part fall into two basic categories. There are the behaviorists whose studies are based on behavior patterns and the effectiveness of changing behavior by repressive means—artificial conditioned reflexes. Then there are those who employ the cognitive approaches based mainly on making the patient 'aware' of behaviors that seemingly are counterproductive to the patient. Janov argues incessantly against all these notions by suggesting there is no permanent real change as long as we ignore the very reason for the malady in the first place. Only Primal Theory, as far as I see, makes any attempt to come up with a reason for the malady. I have seen many arguments refuting Janov's notions, but all seem flimsy and frivolous, the most frequent being that Primal Theory is too simplistic. Until there is a demonstration that nothing simple could ever be correct or valid, I find all those notions mere "sour grapes." Another critique is that it was a 1970s therapeutic fad that proved ineffective. I contend that Janov's insistence on training only by him and his institution and center was the factor that caused the theory to be thrown out with the therapeutic bathwater.

What is psychology?

Psychology, the study of the workings of the mind, is something we humans have toyed with for a very long time. Ignorance of the mechanics of these workings and using the very instrument (the neurotic mind) to look into itself left us without leads for a long time. Shakespeare, I contend, was the great genius and master writer because he intuited why different people saw things in very different ways. His characters were three-dimensional and could often counter the comments of other characters who countered back. Did Shakespeare have some rudimentary understanding of psychology? Perhaps not, but he seemed to have an enormous understanding of people and their feelings and ways of expressing themselves: possibly because he worked in a group-setting, allowing actors imput. That, to me, was his genius and why his works, so many years removed from his style and era, still move and resonate with us.

In the nineteenth century, the medical profession suggested that "madness" was a mental disorder (illness) and attempted to understand it. Eventually, Freud began his study of hysterical women. But even here, the illness was defined through neurophysiology as if a study of the biology of the brain might give us some clues. Without defining neurosis, he contended that it was a factor of being human. Consequently, he was unmindful of what was lost to the subconscious and hoped (forlornly) that becoming "aware" of our history would resolve matters. This, I contend, was why so many splinter groups strayed from the original Freudian notion. Janov suggested that had Freud stayed with the notion that his hysterical patients had been sexually abused by fathers and near relatives, he might have gone in the direction of formulating Primal Theory himself (perhaps under another name). Instead, Freud sought to explain his patients' pathology by suggesting that it was a "deep secret desire" (Oedipus complex) rather than an actual traumatic event in their childhood.

Behaviorism

Concurrent with the development of psychoanalysis, as Freud's work came to be known, a Russian named Ivan Pavlov was beginning to investigate behavior in dogs. Because he was able to stimulate responses artificially and apparently unnaturally, he set out to investigate human behavior in a similar manner through a methodology better known as habit trends. The development of this behaviorism influenced and changed behavior through the mechanism of habit stimuli and punishment. It is remarkable to me that this is now accepted as a scientific approach to psychology. It appears scientific in that we can set up physical parameters of behavior responses and show how they may be affected. What the investigations do not show is *why* or how they are taking place, only that they do take place. This approach leaves us to arbitrarily decide what is and is not amenable to change as I said earlier and merely studies behavior so that we start to look at ourselves (and, sadly, other creatures) through the lens of behavior. Our ability to affect any behavior of any creature by modifying its environment suggests it is an environmental rather than a natural factor and might have some validity in humans if we were unable to fake behavior. Since, I can fake happiness while being miserable and uncomfortable, behavior becomes less reliable as an indicator of my true nature. Furthermore, social behavior in antisocial patients may readily be affected (I contend only temporarily) by the rewards and punishment stimuli, but this situation fails to explain why we were antisocial in the first place. In other words, behaviorists must believe that all human problems result from behavior. But a depressive or psychotic will not cease being either, no matter what we do to affect behavior. I suspect that behaviorism is popular today because it appears tidier.

Several theories had been previously proposed, but the two main ones were behaviorism (à la Pavlov/Skinner) and analysis (à la Freud). There were subdivisions within each of these, but the principles were similar to the originals. The behaviorists had a solid basis for their studies, but in the final analysis were only studying behavior (not the total mind) and not the reason for the behavior and they lacked any real ability to see nature as opposed to behavior. Behavior is not true psychology, but rather "behaviorology." This is perhaps another example of the "lazy-dog" syndrome.

Cognitive therapies

The problem with analysis was the elusiveness of a valid, consistent theory from which to start a real investigation of the subject. I contend the missing link both the professionals and patients have been searching for was discovered when neurosis was defined. Janov had long been frustrated with hodge-podge, hit-or-miss attempts by his profession and so was very diligent after observing (what he called) a reliving event by a patient in a group setting in his office. The event was so unusual and extraordinary that Janov was unwilling to make it fit in to any of his preconceived notions. This demonstrated both his integrity for truth and his genius to admit that for all his 17 years of practice and experience, there was nothing at that time to explain this reliving event.

Primal Theory

If Primal Theory is valid, then the implications for the psychological profession are going to be profound. Maybe this is exactly why the profession is more reluctant than anyone else to accept or even reconsider its validity and efficacy. I contend that anyone who seriously sits down and attempts to invalidate Primal Theory will not succeed. I challenge anyone to make the effort. Opinions and beliefs in the strict scientific sense are not valid reasons for the dismissal of any theory. We need to stay with that theory until we see some invalidation and then, and only then, in all good conscience, dismiss it.

With the advent of Primal Theory, we now have a model through which we can look at all psychological phenomena as well as many other factors. Now it's possible to explain why we feel and respond the way we do, hence we also see why we behave the way we do, the behavior being our response to our feelings. Also, it means we can know why we think the way we do. Just this latter factor helps to explain a great deal about ourselves, particularly in the area we have previously only had "opinions" about.

It is the essence of Primal Theory that feelings are the very basis of our being. If we are free to feel and then express those feelings in one simple and comprehensive whole-feeling event, then the rest of our existence will make sense from within. Furthermore, Primal Theory implies that permitting feelings in the present by responding to them appropriately dislodges the very mechanism that keeps them locked in the subconscious.

These mechanisms are the very defensive systems that have bogged us down and permitted the continuation of this very debilitating illness (neurosis) that has so hounded us for what must be now several millennia. Thus a therapeutic process will already be started merely by permitting a feeling-full environment. This is not to say it is easy or obvious. If we are now able to see where a particular problem arises within ourselves, we may not necessarily be able to correct it, but we could be well on the way to understand it and then perhaps approach a solution. Better still, we would be in a unique position to prevent it in our children.

Consequently, other current psychological theories and modalities come up short on prevention. Again, all we are doing is trying to mend the already damaged. We truly need to prevent neurosis in the first place. Primal Theory overcomes this very problem as I will suggest in the final chapter on child-rearing.

The psychological profession

What this does for the psychological profession is yet another matter. I contend that the profession is far too invested both economically and politically to adapt to change from within. As almost always, change is brought about in most spheres when the population at large begins to accept a general principle. Copernicus and Galileo are a case in point. The change for the mental health care profession will come from the outside, as it did with the Church.

In summary:

Cognitive psychotherapy is engaged in diagnosing.

Behavioral therapy is engaged in repressing.

Psychiatry is engaged in medicating.

Primal Therapy is engaged in feeling.

18

Economics

trying to control a symbol

The study of economics is about money flow: money is not static. However, our general understanding of "economics" refers normally to the management of money, but we can use the same word for the management of time, energy and resources. Economics also relies heavily on value, but what indicates value? No two people have the same value for anything. It is really a value judgment. Money only pretends to give a value. I would like to add another factor that we could look at economically and that is the economy of our desires—what we need to pay (not necessarily money) in order to fulfill our desires, i.e. the consequences of pursuing and achieving our desires.

As stated above, economics usually refers to money and its management, but money is a symbol and as such we are involved with the management of a symbol. In its simplest aspects, the management of money in a family, small business or small community situation is as simple as money flow in, balanced against money flow out. The budget is considered balanced if the two are relatively equal. However, this is not how modern economics operates now in either the corporate world or governments; both are manipulations to simulate the flow of money around. What is really taking place is the manipulation of a symbol. We neurotics have made money the means of control, against our better nature, which I will elaborate on later.

The process has become so complex that even the experts do not have a total grasp of it and is now seem more guess work than a science. What we now are involved in is the process of lending, borrowing, buying, selling and hedging, derivatives, collateralized debt obligations, index funds, credit default swaps and investment vehicles. Borrowing has become the means to augment one's assets, but in order to borrow, one needs to show the potential to repay. Herein is the catch: few meet that requirement, only the priv-

eleged few. Of course, there was always a risk and the money lenders calcu-
lated the risks to offset their potential losses. Not only do businesses use this
methodology, but also governments have gotten into it and the whole house
of cards (we are dealing with symbols) is likely to collapse sometime in the
very near future. We are stretching the system to its limit with ever-newer
ideas about how to overcome money turnover slow-down. The current
mortgage debacle is a case in point.

The Economics of Desire

The economics of desires is something we neurotics hardly ever contemplate, but we must weigh the benefits of getting our desires met against
the consequences involved in achieving those desires. Our desires are a direct result of our feelings. Children understand all this intuitively. I contend
all living creatures understand this on some full-feeling level. We neurotics
have enmeshed ourselves in sophisticated economic notions which lead us
to think in terms of value instead of seeing it directly through the consequences of our desires. *"was it really worth aquiring?"*

Additionally, we need to consider the economics of resources in order
to get a better grasp of what we really mean by economics. I suggest that the
greatest resource any nation has is its population. A potential work force is a
dynamic resource were we able to harness it. Were the poorer nations of this
world able to mobilize their populations to become productive and at the
same time feed them, house them and take care of basic needs, such that we
did not need some symbol (money) to moderate it, we might see a process
that could accelerate upon itself and as their goods and services became sta-
ble enough, they would establish self-sufficient communities. In the past this
idea was greatly considered, (Prudhen, Marx etc.) but neurotic governance
dismissed it outright. I will expand on this idea in the chapter on politics.

Definition of economics

"The dictionary defines economic as the management of one's business,
source of income and expenditures in an orderly, methodical, hence thrifty
manner. I would prefer that we define it as the flow of money (the means of
exchange), but as is being demonstrated in the current economic meltdown,
is that the money flow is slowing down. Governments are now being compelled to stimulate a speeding up of the money flow. In a laissey faire mar-

ket system this leaves too much to chance. Even a centralized sytem, as was/is the case in both Russia and China it's more chance than certainty.

Value is a judgment, not a universal set state. By what standard do we dictate value? No two neurotics place the same value on anything; hence we have "value judgment." In the macro-environment of money flow, i.e. that of governments or large corporations, economics has become so complex that it now requires a degree from a university to merely understand all the complexities. In the early days, some centuries ago, we started to manipulate the process by borrowing the difference, then paying interest on that borrowed money, especially if the borrowed money was able to create more money. The day of reckoning came when the borrowed money (principal) needed to be paid back by whatever means—Shylock in Shakespeare's *The Merchant of Venice*. It was at this point that there was an attempt to manipulate this situation to especially benefit the borrower. One way was to devalue the principal; another was to sell that loan by way of what we now consider stock. Now with hedge funds and other financial manipulations, we have a very complex situation that even experts have only a periferal understanding of, hence the automatic uncertainty of stocks causing crashes and market collapses. Now governments are using the very same principle, borrowing fast to keep a spending spree going that makes the supposed overall economy *appear* as if it's in good shape. The Reagan administration began to use this to great effect due to the ideas promulgated by Margaret Thatcher of Britain thought out by Milton Friedman and the Chicago School. There is a catch here and the Bush administration has now taken this to its extreme by borrowing big time. Not to run the American social system, but to run the military-industrial complex. The lenders are beginning to catch on and seemingly, quite soon, going to stop lending. This will throw the whole world economy into a scramble and we'll be left with a no-fix situation for anyone. Borrowers will renege on the debt and lenders will refuse to lend and the ultimate symbol will come crashing around us.

The economics of matters other than money.

So instead of the simple balanced system of what goes out equals what comes in, we now find ourselves trying to make some sense of more complexity and the need to make it into a science. We study some very complex statistics to make some sort of sense out of it all. Studying the economy of time or resources teaches us the obvious: time and resources do not generate interest. As I stated earlier, the greatest resource that any nation has—or the world community for that matter—is its people and their energy. Were we able to mobilize that resource, I contend we could eliminate hunger, provide food shelter and health care around the globe. All that would be required is that in the interim, we would need to feed, house and take care of children, the old and the infirm until such time as the mobilization became self-inducing and sufficient.

It is my contention that if the richer countries of the world were to help the poorer nations through a transitional period, while those third-world nations utilized the population at large, by way of bottom up governanance, we could see a multiplying effect so that eventually these smaller nations would then help the larger nations through their own transition. Alas, the very opposite has happened and the United States in particular has hindered with its blind faith in market forces, every socialist revolution on the planet in its own attempt to maintain its economic power and privilege.

Economics of desires could replace morality.

If we were to look into the nature of desires (wants) and use our concept of economics in choosing what we desire, I feel we would see clearer ideas of how to manage our desires. Since our desires stem from our feelings about what we would like (as opposed to need), attempting to fulfill our desires would naturally help us to understand the effort needed to bring that about. It has been our failure (because of neurosis) to see that this replaces a need for morality (righteousness/wrongteousness). In reverse, we probably created morality to substitute for the economy of desire at the point of becoming neurotic when we lost our native understanding of the consequences of our desires. Far too often, our current capitalist system and our current understanding of the economy (money) blind us to what I am calling "the economics of desire." What is the point of allowing ourselves to become maladapted or ill in order to obtain something? Do we neurotics allow ourselves to fully grasp the question: "Is it worth it" in the quality of life sense? Most of the time, we do not.

We tend to solve our frustrations and problems by attempting to change the outward aspects of what seemingly is thwarting the desires. For example, if only the other person or situation would change, then our desires would be met. As any smart philosopher knows, it is simply a matter of looking into ourselves, our desires and our ability to suffer our frustrations, rather than to *blame* others or outside forces on our inability to get what we want hence, I would like to suggest an economy of desires to replace the economy of money. This in turn would negate the need for morality (right v wrong). The religious amongst us will not see this, much less accept it.

The nature of exchange

In earlier times, we bartered which inevitably led us to create the symbol of money to avoid carrying around those things needed for bartering. We do not need to consider going back to a barter system. That was part of the neurotic capitalist process anyway.

Exchange is not intrinsic to our nature, but giving and/or taking, without evaluating (giving value to) what is given for what is received, are intrinsic. If we are able to give freely and can accept without evaluating, then a major part of the guilt that abounds in the giving and taking process could be eliminated. Then we might begin to see the madness of our current economic system. "It's the only system we have and the only system we could have." This is yet another of our neurotic myths.

The greed factor: the beast within us. Beasts, incidently, never are greedy, but only ever hungry. Once their hunger is appeased, they are content and not even a threat to any other creature. They feel a sense of "live and let live," something we humans seemingly have to learn cognitively.

Since happiness is not pursuable, then I would like to suggest that the pre-amble to the American Constitution should have read: "Life, liberty and the pursuit of greed." It certainly encapsulates what takes place here in the United States and made readily available in the rich mans casino; the stock market.

Cheating the monetary system

Gambling is the pursuit of something for nothing. As stated by Michael Philips in *Seven Laws of Money*, money has its own rules and you don't exactly have money given and you never actually are able to give it away. One may, on getting money, eliminate some problems related to not having enough (whatever 'enough' is supposed to mean), but often misunderstand the problems that come with acquiring it. Giving money is also never simple and has agendas. Earning money actually follows this same principle.

The Bangladeshi Nobel-prize economist Muhammad Yunus (Grameen Bank) demonstrated that small loans to poor people are effective and 98% repaid. I wonder if the repayment percentage is as high for other loans. This goes against the trend of the big lenders that only want to lend to large and purportedly safe organizations. If this trend from Muhammad Yunus would catch on, we could possibly reverse the current economic tendency that makes the rich richer while repressing the poor and disenfranchised.

An alternative

I reiterate, the greatest economic resource of any nation is its population. Since in all major countries it seems acceptable to live on borrowed money, why not make a change in national policy? Invest in people (as opposed to the corporations) and put them to tasks (work) and provide them with the essentials in order to survive: food, rudimentary shelter and basic healthcare. At the same time let them run the companies/organisations they are involved in. I feel this type of investment in their population would start a process that would begin to uplift the people and the national economy. It might also presage a cooperative lifestyle for these nations. It is becoming obvious that the World Trade Organization (WTO) has not achieved what it set out to: a bolstering of the economies of third-world nations. Instead, the major receipts go back into large corporations of first-world nations and third-world nations merely finish up with a large debt that they are unable to repay—the madness of the notion that market forces create a simple and natural regulating factor—the deep rooted creado of Milton Freidman Chicago School and the political right.

The absurdity of the economics of money is apparent when and if we try to apply the same principle to time or resources. We cannot borrow time. Even if we could we would not be able to pay interest on it!

Our better nature

I suggested in the earlier part of this chapter that the desire to control through the means of an exchange system (money) was against our better feeling-full nature. There are two good reasons for this. The first is that "value" is not a constant from one human to another. The second is that "exchange" is not intrinsic to our being either—giving and separtely receiving are. In order to circumvent this we neurotics created a sense of morality and then tried to justify all this by inventing a deity that begat religion; the subject of my next chapter.

19

Religion
the root of all evil

Religion is the root of all evil because it was the religious mind-set that created the concepts of good and evil. That's the dichotomy (splitting into two), but one man's *good* is another man's *evil*. Good and/or evil are value judgments. Righteousness is not a characteristic out there in the ether although religion imbued us with that notion.

Religiosity is an act of believing. For the most part, what we are asked to believe defies logic since there is no intrinsic basis for religious belief. It is nearly always taught to us in childhood and mostly inculcated through fear, even including those agnostics who survive without any deep religious feeling into old age, then on nearing death, get scared and jump onto the "everlasting" bandwagon, just in case …

Let's look at the act of belief. We actually "know" or "don't know." Believing is an attempt to create a third factor beyond the dichotomy—an attempt to find a middle course. We neurotics, having devised a middle course (belief), now try to make this middle course closer to "knowing" rather than to "not knowing." So, to bolster the rhetoric, we call believing an act of faith. We are asked to "have faith" as if that now justifies believing.

Another word in common use surrounding belief systems is "spirituality." I contend this is yet another attempt by neurotics to justify believing when in fact we do not know. I feel that neurotics, in their subliminal awareness, know there is something above and beyond what we call consciousness. It is this which impels us towards some belief system which we term spirituality and we have done this since we became neurotic. This, I contend, is the neurotics' attempt to grasp and explain the subliminal awareness of the subconscious.

Through this thinking process, we tend to acquire cultural answers. However, these are not monolithic: many of us diverge from one another in our moral codes. There are no two people that I have met whose moral code list is exactly the same, yet it is assumed we all agree, but on closer look we don't. In the final analysis, morality boils down to a matter of opinion—something ethicists grapple with—which might demonstrate the incongruity of morality.

Good and/or evil

At the beginning of this chapter, I postulated the creation of the concept of good and evil. There is no intrinsic concept of good and evil, right and wrong, until we start to judge other people's actions. Strangely, most of us never think of ourselves as either good or evil, but we do hope that others think of us as good (our ego). It is in this sense that good and evil are a dichotomy: setting our judgments one way or another. Why don't we just say "I like this" or "I don't like that"? Why do we seek a universal category (righteousness) of some action or other? Here I have just presented the dialectic—the art of disputation, of reasoning about matters of opinion. We neurotics too often presume a universality of good or evil, yet fail to recognize that we are all different and so are our definitions about what is good and what is evil. Recently, General Peter Pace (an American Marine Corps general, Joint Chief of Staff) suggests that homosexuality is morally evil based on the same premise as "thou shalt not commit adultery," but this very same general is promoting killing (his profession), and fails to take note of the commandment "Thou shalt not kill." A very convenient moral lapse and a gross act of hypocrisy.

The God concept

The nature of God: First: he (or she, or it as some have suggested) is all-powerful. If he is omnipotent, why did he create us with the propensity to become sinners? The usual believers' retort is to say that he also gave us free will. Why did he give us free will if most of us abuse that free will, often to our own detriment? Second: he is benevolent. If benevolent, then why does he allow all the horrors of the world to take place? Most of these horrors seemingly fly in the face of a benevolent creator. Third: he takes care of us individually—the concept of a single being ever capable of intimately taking care of six billion of us! Fourth: he requires us to worship him. Does not psychology suggest that the need to be worshipped is an egocentric act? Fifth: he doles out punishment to sinners, contradicting the benevolent notion. Did not Jesus, his son, suggest that we love our enemies? Our only understanding of him (God) comes from scriptures written many centuries ago with little or no valid authentication or any real understanding of their proponents. The scriptures are of very questionable historic authenticity and if read from cover to cover, offer a very divisive and war-like narrative of the periods. If language was a part of our evolution, then writing was even more recent than speaking and in its earliest form very imprecise. Why is it assumed that ancient writings any more authentic than ancient thinking at a time when humans assumed the earth was flat? A book by Ben Akerley, *The X-Rated Bible*, makes this point very succinctly.

Who is God?

I contend, in the Primal Theory context, religion tries to explain the inexplicable. If we were just aware of the subconscious and its contents, I feel we would never have cause or concern for explaining anything we did not fully understand. Believing (a verb) is crazy. We either know or we don't know. The more neurotic we became the more we needed a morality as we lost the ability to see the econonomy of our desires. Having created a morality we created a diety to justify that morality and explaining that subliminal feeling *in the basck of our minds*. We created a God in our own neurotic image.

Rites, rituals and religion

If there was a God, there wouldn't be any atheists. We would instinctively know of its/her/his existence. If this God was in the business of punishing, then atheists would get short shrift for their offense. The real question is: Why has God kept himself in hiding for most of our known human history and even now—with all the technological advances—still hiding? Why is it necessary to have missionaries? Why is it not instinctual to accept his existence and nature? Why do we have to be taught about God and why do all three major monotheisms differ so widely, each claiming to have "the truth"?

Why do we make reference to this God as "father"? There is something very Freudian here. Surely we could give him a better title. The other title we give him is the old aristocratic "Lord" and we often refer to Jesus as "King." Is not all this some remnant of our capitalist hierarchical system?

"Honor thy mother and father" is perhaps the most neurotic of the commandments. This has been a means to deprive children throughout time

of their most instinctual feelings ever. Deep down, each child knows the
extent of love (or lack of it) from their parents, but this one commandment
so profusely invoked (by parents invariably) is depriving children of their
own feelings and hence knowledge of their caregivers. It is insidious. Children owe nothing to their parents. Parents ought to have instincts to nurture
and love their offspring unconditionally. How many of us ex-children are
imbued with guilt about what we owe and should give to our parents? From
this guilt stems perhaps our greatest degree of the shame of ourselves, of
our parents, of our very being.

Religion is conceived in the mind—a head trip—it is not instinctive, intuitive or intrinsic. What is actually instinctive is something deeper within
ourselves that seems remote and inexplicable. I contend because the subconscious is inaccesable we neurotically try to explain it. It is these explanations that create the complex notions of a god, a creator, a reason for life,
etc.

Morality

Certainly morality is not instinctive either. We all deep down know what
we like and don't like. Why do we have to turn that into some moralistic
notion of right and/or wrong?

Some religious rituals are: prayer, singing praise, worship of a father figure, belief in life beyond this one. Prayer is about the best way of talking to
ourselves, yet allowing us to feel we are talking to someone else. Singing and
praise are just another outlet for celebrating and enjoying life (Afro-
American churches do this best)—why must there be a God pretext? A life
in the hereafter implies hope for a second chance—this one was not so
good after all?

The Primal raison d'être.

Religion seen in the primal context is the best way (without understanding the nature of the subconscious) to explain it. In the back of our mind we
harbor a feeling that there is something, but we know not what. Marvin Harris suggests in *Cows, Pigs, Wars and Witches* that all these rites, rituals and relig-
ions are merely mundane economic factors—ways to keep the community
cohesive and viable. Without neurosis there would be no necessity for any
belief system.

We need only look at the history of our human development of religion from totem poles to current monotheisms, to the god within (Buddhism). What we are doing is trying to explain that subliminal sense we have of the subconscious.

Judaism left us with the legacy of the Ten Commandments and the notion of a chosen people—a self-fulfilling prophecy if ever there was one—an "eye for an eye... ." as a primitive injunction. Christianity attempted to update that with "...let him smite thee on the other cheek" and claimed the messiah had come and gone. Islam and the (less conceited) prophet notion also updated Judaism. Buddhism attempted to put God within us, and despite being a much less neurotic concept, still failed to recognize that it was in our subconscious.

Religious types

There are basically three types of religious followers and within the three types, three subtypes:

The scripturists

a) Those who believe the scriptures are the actual word of God. (How come this all-powerful creature can't write or, for that matter speak certainly in any recognizable tongue?)

b) Those who believe the writers were divinely inspired and wrote for God. (Who designated whom to be divinely inspired?)

c) Those who believe they are allegorical.

The worshippers

a) Those who believe he needs to be worshipped (otherwise he will not let us into his kingdom).

b) Those who believe the need to praise him for all the good he gave us (but never blame him for all the bad).

c) Those who believe it is a communal gathering to celebrate him. (What's wrong with just enjoying and experiencing the gathering?)

The prayer makers

a) Those who believe in ritualistic prayer (reciting the Lord's Prayer) without having to know what it really means).

b) Those who believe we can ask for our desires (pray to curry favors).

c) Those who believe in communion with their higher power (little realizing that they are their own higher power if they could eliminate their neurosis).

Fundamentalism

Fundamentalists are normally scripturists who believe that the scriptures are the exact words of God, the creator, but acknowledge they were written by fellow sinners (neurotics), gaining popularity when they came close to a collective subconscious reasoning.

Some suggest that we humans have morality hard-wired into us. I disagree. Righteousness and wrongteousness are mere value judgments that we are taught very early in childhood. We know what we like and we know what we don't like; we neurotics make our likes good and our dislikes bad (evil). Since medieval times the Church has lost its grip on the populace and so as it slipped from its power pinnacle, we needed another institution to keep the populace in order. This is where government in the modern sense began to take hold; hence we have politics.

Athesim/Humanism/Sectarianism

Jonathon Miller in his three part BBC television program *A Brief History of Disbelief* suggested that atheism was yet another belief system and certainly the promotion of atheism/humanitarianism/sectarianism seems to bear out that notion. Rationl thinking as a counter to religion never did, nor ever will pursued 'believers' to abandon their belief system. Their believing is a part of their neurosis, but then believing/indulging in rational thinking, logic or science is also part of our neurosis. So might politics overcome this dichotomy? This is my next chapter.

20

Politics

(the need to be guided)

There is basically only one political system: capitalism. The alternative is to be apolitical (have no politics), often referred to as "anarchy," meaning without a hierarchical system. Sadly, the word "anarchy" has come to signify chaos and chaos to signify fear. This is not a true state of affairs. There are many chaotic situations that are even pleasurable: nature, for one, and many more that we take for granted such as the weather. It may be considered that I left out communism, but as conceived by Karl Marx, it was actually an attempt to transition from a capitalist system to an anarchic one, i.e. without law, without government, without money. We neurotics find it very hard to conceive of a system without money and feel if *others* were left with no incentive to earn, nothing would ever get achieved. This myth is dispelled when we consider the many who volunteer services for free when all their other needs are met.

Since we humans started out without any political system, way back when (misconceived as a time of great tyranny), we were just simply living the life. So why did we bring about, however slowly, the complicated system we have today? I contend that with the advent and development of neurosis, we invented a hierarchy to control the *assumed* uncontrollable mob. It was a slowly evolving process, first through tribes and tribal leaders and then on to our current systems of monarchy, dictatorship and so-called democracy.

We talk glibly about democracy and a democratic system and yet there is no democracy in the home: it is a dictatorship (usually daddy). There is no democracy in the school: it is a dictatorship (usually the teacher). There is no democracy in the workplace: it is dictatorship (usually the boss). If in all these situations everyone had equal say, we might achieve real democracy. Democratic governance by the people does not actually exist. What we have instead is "representational democracy" which in effect means we express our democratic feeling on Election Day only—invariably ill informed—the rest of the time, it is a sort of dictatorship by committee. Either way, it is always controlled by capital (money), which is controlled by big business. Of course, in order to make this control effective, we need rules which become laws which in turn beget repression. All laws are basically "thou shalt not…"

The beginning of politics

Anarchy and chaos are something we neurotics have abhorred since they appeared some centuries ago, yet we have lived with them throughout time in one form or another. Our fear is not realistic, but rather grounded in neurotic concepts: childhood fear.

Though we know almost nothing about human social life earlier than 10,000 years ago, there is little doubt that we have evolved. What we evolved from is hard to ascertain if we merely stay with concepts of mankind as being an utterly distinct, thinking species. In the chapter on The Nature of Thinking, I suggested that before we could think, we were more akin to other mammals, especially the apes and monkeys. If it can be ascertained that neurosis was something we acquired at some given moment in time, then we might come up with some reason for it. We will then have surmounted a great obstacle to current concepts of our beginnings. Whatever that was—and there are some conjectures—it remains true that our development into neurosis led us down the path to local (tribal) leaders.

These early primitive leaders were accepted by the community and that factor, I contend, contributed to the early neurosis. The problem with such a disease is that it does not stay dormant, but forever reverberates and becomes more deeply engrained into the community. I contend that as a result of this, the population grew larger causing space (territory) to become scarce, perhaps leading to territorial fights with neighbors and the beginnings of the tribal feuds. Thus we, in our early neurotic state, began a process that has led us to our present-day situation. We transitioned from the tribal leader to the conqueror that created an even larger tribe needing more vigorous control resulting in the beginnings of what we now know as nations with police and armies.

This created city states and then larger states and, eventually, today's large nations. We humans are somewhat aware of larger entities developing; now we have federations and the beginnings of a world government, although maybe not realized in my lifetime. Trade certainly is being globalized and it is not too far fetched to imagine a world government giving states (countries) the right to deal with national issues only.

Utopian is not a valid criticism

In the meantime, we have not resolved our neurotic, selfish greed, and we hold on to privilege perpetuated with subconscious need (rather than real need) for survival. It is no accident that the notion of anarchy (without hierarchy) has only been conceived by some of the more feeling-full amongst us. It's a pity there is not enough of a critical mass who have thought this principle through. I both feel and hope that an understanding of Primal Theory might facilitate this notion and eventually encourage a critical mass into understanding it. It is my feeling that only youth might be prepared to go there. I feel sure a revolutionary surge would then occur to implement it.

The major critique is that it is idealistic, utopian and/or simplistic. Why idealistic and/or utopian and/or simplistic are unacceptable is not reasonable or logical. We have prejudged these words as emotional and unacceptable. I hope that an understanding of Primal Theory will convince the populace, or at least youth, that simplicity is what we should be striving for instead of complexity—feelings instead of thinking. The greatest concept out of Hawking's *A Brief History of Time* is simplicity, which we are going to have to eventually achieve if we are going to survive as a species.

Meanwhile, we are left believing representational democracy is our best means of governance. Nowhere is there real government by the people— from the bottom up. What we have currently perpetuates corruption and special interests from small groups that are determined to maintain their privilege. Without the understanding of Primal Theory, the majority neurosis becomes what we all have to abide by. We call this democracy and worse, consider it "civilized"; rule by a majority is in and of itself neurotic.

Gradations of neurosis

Though neurosis abounds, there are gradations of it. The more damaged in childhood some of us were, the more neurotic we are likely to be. This shows up most clearly in the professions that some of us have chosen. The following, I contend, are the least feeling-full and most neurotic: police, prison guards, armed forces (the military), animal experimenters and politicians.

Sadly, any form of government will inevitably lead to corruption. Corruption will not be eliminated until we can make privilege irrelevant. Privilege creates all the inequalities like racism, sexism, ageism, etc. We see this best in the United States where Caucasian males attempt to hang on to their privileges with some of the most convoluted laws, especially those of the United States Constitution, created by male Anglo-Saxons. The declaration permitting the pursuit of happiness is an oxymoron because feelings are not pursuable. They happen to us willy-nilly.

Why the United States politics?

I talk about the United States political system here to make my point, but in actuality all political systems fit in to this hypocritical incongruity. The defense system of any state (should be called an "offense system") is a tactical pursuit to bully some lesser states into submission and maintain the larger states' privileges. The United States inaugurated this very policy and maintains it to this very day. Israel has done this to the Palestinians with aid and privilege from U. S. taxpayers, without which Israel would perhaps never have come into being in the first place because of the West's guilt complex over the Holocaust. We hide this bullying tactic under the name of "security" which is a major oxymoron actually creating the very insecurity we hope to prevent, something neurotics are very prone to do without understanding what it achieves.

Illegality of drugs

One of the great absurdities of nearly all governments is their repressive nature by criminalizing painkilling (hardcore) drugs. Some of our more traditional ones like alcohol and tobacco still remain legal, but are rapidly beginning to be seen as harmful. Now we see governments dictating to their people which painkillers are or are not reasonable (legal). In many cases criminalization of drugs chosen to medicate, causes further complications in both a social and criminal justice system which are equally unjust and irrational. Justification for this practice is premised on protecting people from addiction without recognizing that, one way or another, all neurotics (all of us) indulge in addictive practices; therefore, criminalizing any addiction is self-defeating. Addictive practices eventually distract from the quality of life, but who is to say which of them are better or worse? Why are we not (individually) allowed to decide and be sovereign unto ourselves?

The most dangerous aspect of illegal painkilling drugs is procuring them, not using them. A human without subconscious pain could not, by definition, become addicted to anything. Neurotic governance seemingly cannot grasp this concept and thus we are left with "a drug problem" or worse still "a war on drugs" that is inevitably unwinnable.

Many Americans are beginning to understand that the United States political system is badly broken. There are many suggestions (usually political) as to how to fix it. I suggest that none of them will succeed because the very problem is the nature of governance in and of itself which explains why the solution is not possible through politics. The United States Constitution is now more than 200 years old and was at its inception merely a continuation of that which it broke away from—made tidier. It broke away from a relatively free nation. The creation of a president merely replaced a lifetime monarch with a supreme-powered politician. In hindsight, a political head of state potentially invites more abuse. The U. S. currently has this very state of affairs, but trying to fix it with a flawed constitution is like trying to repair the car when it's totaled—it is better to start from scratch. We glibly talk of freedom and yet we in the West consider "representational democracy" the closest we will ever get to it. Janov in *Prisoner of Pain* suggests all neurotics are prisoners. If this is so, then the only real freedom is the freedom to feel. All other freedoms are therefore and thereafter irrelevant. The absurdity of government is its perpetual attempt to fix problems which never really get fixed. We need to rethink all this and contemplate the idea of abolishing top-down governance altogether. Possibly one solution could be allowing the workers to run their own workplaces (democratically) along with the community where the workplace is located. This idea is already in process in Argentine. Another might be the nationalization of all land and all natural resources. Then let the workers be in charge of them. This one idea could eliminate many of the inequality problems of all states and governments. I call this the "decorporatization" of business.

Addictive substances

In the chapter on Medicine I touched on the nature of addiction and its ramifications. Here I would like to develop that theme and talk about the legality/illegality of addictive substances—drugs. There are two types of illegal mood elevators. The first consists of those that promote feeling-fullness: lysergic acid (LSD), marijuana and some mushrooms, primarily peyote, then those that suppress feelings: heroin and the opiates cocaine and crack cocaine and the amphetamines. It has been argued that the attempt to keep hardcore drugs illegal actually creates the very problem that governments are intent on trying to prevent. The best example was prohibition of alcohol in the United States during the 1920s. Making them legal would allow a serious discussion about their real dangers and would allow for the relative safety of their manufacture and distribution. Then pharmaceutical and government factions could label and warn buyers of these substances to give some idea what their ingestion is *actually* doing. Alas, the current thinking on this matter is another example of our "nine-dot syndrome" thinking. We are unable to get out of the 'box' we trapped ourselves into.

The political divide

There is a general feeling in the United States that the electorate has wisdom in choosing its leaders and hence the legislation that ensues. I predict the so-called election of George W. Bush will eliminate that myth forever. A collective neurosis is no more valid than an individual one.

It would be an easy matter to suggest ways out of our current political predicament (as did Karl Marx), but I feel strongly that this is a matter we need to try somewhat collectively and with a great deal of debate. It will inevitably be a slow process, but will only occur when it is generally accepted that what we have, and the direction we are currently going, are not working. I suggest that this would be an evolutionary process among all the peoples of the planet and not any particular elite group. My (neurotic) hope is that this, my book, might start the process.

Fascists, Republicans, neo-conservatives, conservatives and right-wing politicos, are usually people with a predominant (subconscious) anger from childhood and were punished for their anger and now see punishment as the means to control others, hence they lean to thinking of punishment mostly as the means of effective control—mainly of others. This accounts for believing in capital punishment, incarceration, corporal punishment and punishment of children, a sort of backwards way of justifying what happened to themselves in childhood. Their other credo is that *market forces* are a naturally contolling faculty—myth. The neo-conservative principle of imbuing upon the populous their notion of morality through their religious affiliation seeks to control that populace with its elite group that perpetuate this religious morality, while they, the elite know better. Sadly this very same notion is promulgated by the Islamic, so called, terrorists groups like the Al Quada.

It's the same idea based on its religious morality.   The only difference are the two moralities. Both, in Primal terms are neurotic.

Anarchists, socialists, labor unionists and environmentalists are usually people that have a lot of sadness as their primal pain and feel what happened to them was unjust and unfair, hence they lean towards a more compassionate means of governing, connecting the present system with their unjust past.

As a consequence our current political thinking and ideas are predetermined by subliminal (subconscious) feelings. All this suggests that we were hard-wired into our political ideas and opinions during those formative years and not that we had any fundamental or intellectual opinions or rationale about them later in life. The reverse is true: our old pain determines present-day opinions, thinking and ideas. Most neurotics will find this very hard to consider, least of all accept.

Roveian rhetoric (Karl Rove) is an outgrowth of a right-wing mind-set determined to win by spin, distortion and catch phrases. This only works in situations where the electorate has little interest in thoughtful debate (which requires time and energy) and so the electorate accepts quick slogans and clichés that have some subliminal resonance, hence the 30 second sound bite.

Dmetri Orlov, a Russian national that lived in and through the fall of the Soviet Union, suggests that the inevitable fall of capitalism (very imminent he says) will create an even worse scenario for the people of the Western world. I agree with that. So is there a philosophical fix? That is my next chapter.

21

Philosophy

by what principles can we live?

Definition: the love of wisdom—the disipline that studies the realities of human nature and searches for the reason and nature of things

Religion, politics and philosophy are actually the same mind-set. Each is trying to explain how we should live, according to someone else's idea how to do so. Descartes said, "I think, therefore I am." I would like to change that in view of Primal Theory and say "I feel, therefore I be." This approach, I contend, delves deeper into our nature (rather than our behavior) and suggests that we are a more basic creature than we have hitherto admitted.

Philosophy connotes a search for wisdom, but without defining what constitutes being wise. It leaves us floundering as it endeavors to understand the realities of human nature. I contend that any real understanding of our nature could not be realized before Primal Theory, since all we were doing before was confusing nature with behavior, creating several schools of thought on the matter without knowing quite why. To fully-feel negates any reason to ponder what or why; we just merely experience ourselves within our environment. Put another way, we each of us can only live within the bubble of our own feelings.

In more recent times, it has become acceptable that some of us have our own philosophy. Most of our ideas are based on our cultural values and belief systems. Philosophy came last in our thinking development, perhaps giving it pseudo-nobleness. I again feel this is a factor of our neurosis. If we were fully-feeling creatures without neurosis, I contend we would neither need religion (a need to believe) nor politics (a need to follow) nor philosophy (a need to have a route to follow).

If we put rats into a box with pegs and holes and different channels that they may investigate, we could very well study their behavior in that environment and in those circumstances. This is not a real investigation into their nature. For that we would need to follow these creatures in their most natural settings, something science and scientists find impractical.

All studies of humans that do not take Primal Theory into account are tantamount to studying ourselves in the neurotic box just as we have done with the aforementioned rats. We have never been able to view or study human nature, merely behavior in the box of our own creation.

If, on the other hand, we are only concerned with our own philosophy and individual conduct of our own lives, we need to be equally aware of our nature as opposed to our behavior. Only after an extensive period of my own therapy and ensuing insights was I able to discover what I needed to know about myself. I came up with the following:

First, to know myself by:-

a) Knowing what I like (the good) about myself.

b) Knowing what I do not like (the bad) about myself.

c) Knowing what I positively hate (the downright ugly) about myself.

Then, after I knew myself (my real self), had to decide what I really wanted. That took many more insights.

Once I knew what I wanted, I next needed to know how to get it. This was/is the hardest part. Had I not been damaged (traumatized in childhood), I feel this would have all been very natural from my birth and I would have known naturally who I was. The very process of life (especially in childhood) would have taught me how to achieve all this without having to resort to hurting or using others deliberately or unwittingly.

There are some of us who know the good, or hope we know the good, about ourselves. It is the egotist within us that prevents us from seeing either the bad, or worse, the downright ugly. Then there are those who only know the bad about themselves—usually those with little self-esteem. Then there are the severely depressed who only see the very ugly about themselves. The latter often need extensive psychotherapy or, at some level, institutionalization. There are gradations for all of these, but they tend to fall into the rough categories I have just laid out.

Until we are able to see our whole selves, we will neurotically strive with our ego to see only what we want to see and hence inhibit ourselves in knowing who we truly are, and what we want. The problem with wanting is that in the pursuit of our wants (desires), we often fail to take into consideration the resulting consequences—*the economy of desire.*

All we need to know

Perhaps one of the greatest pieces of wisdom that I am aware of comes (supposedly) out of the mouth of Jesus when he said, "It is written, an eye for an eye and tooth for a tooth, but I say unto ye, if he smite thee on the one cheek, turn, and let him smite thee on the other." I contend that here Jesus was taking an old covenant from Judaism and updating it, which suggests not all the covenants had validity in his eyes. Ironically, most of us—modern Israelis being no exception—seem bent on several eyes for one eye and many teeth for one tooth, in contravention to that covenant. Furthermore, Jesus, in this preaching, was subtly suggesting that in offering the other cheek, we resolve more than 99% of our conflicts and confrontations. I have tried this on some occasions and been quite surprised that it takes the power away from my aggressors. I feel this is little realized or understood among the Christian clergy, let alone the greater Christian community and I see no sign that the Christian Right understands anything about the philosophical implications or wisdom here.

Another is the purported saying "Suffer the little children to come unto me for theirs is the kingdom of heaven." Presuming that children are in heaven—it is we adults that are in hell. Did Jesus have some precursor to Primal Theory?

In summary, I am suggesting that all we need to know is who we are, what we want and how to get it. All else is extraneous. Alas, having tied ourselves to the principle of morality, we deprive ourselves of the ability to search for the real self as we are forever striving to believe we are nearer nirvana (perfection) than we really are. Giving up such a belief is what we neurotics are most reluctant to do. So where might we go from here?

Part III

Transformation to a Non-Neurotic World

Part II may seem depressing, but the current political climate is not very conducive to an optimistic outlook anyway. Part II also attempts to "slaughter many sacred cows." I hope the following part III can offer some way we might (just might) prevent what to my mind is a path to total disaster for us humans and the planet which I predict before the end of this century.

It is almost impossible to know what life would be like in a non-neurotic (feeling-full) world, but that does not mean that we cannot conjecture. The following chapters, with the exception of Childrearing, are merely a conjecture of this. No doubt, as time passes and ideas start to circulate, we may see some adaptation as to what it could entail. Some of the things we have invented and discovered we might still enjoy for our and other species' greater comfort. I doubt that we would want to give up the use of language as a means of communicating with one another and even the ability to travel (roam the planet freely). However, I doubt that travel would be excessive, whereas forms of communication, especially in light of the computer, internet and e-mail, would coalesce and we might find an incentive towards a common language and means of communication based on feelings.

Here in the last part are my feelings about how we just might be able to reverse the direction we humans have pursued for the last several millennia. There is no "how to" here, merely my feelings, suggestions and conjectures. It is my wish it might help parents, and particularly mothers, in the rearing of their children and preventing some of the awesome pain that causes the neurosis in their offspring in the first place, but I feel it will take more than just one generation to eliminate neurosis. All else, I contend, serves merely as "band-aids."

Part III deals with a conjecture of how we humans might make the transformation to a feeling-full world. I offer it, not as the only possibility, but rather as an inspiration for what it just might be like. It is not a utopia in the normal sense of that word because we would not be ridding ourselves of sadness, anger, fear, tragedy, or accidents, but we could minimize many of the more unlikable feelings.

We neurotics tend to over complicate our feeling with; being afraid to be frightened, irritated at being angry or grief stricken at being sad. Can we not just be frightened, angry or sad ... simply? We could make life a great deal simpler and certainly more understandable.

22

Without Culture

Community in a non-neurotic world

If culture is a result of our rites, rituals and religious background, could we and would we be willing to live without it? It might be hard for many of us to grasp the implications of what this means or even feels like. I contend that it would give all of us sovereignty over ourselves and be a great advantage to know that we do not need the ideas and feelings of others (including our family, friends and teachers) to manipulate us. We could become completely self-sufficient unto our individual selves.

In a fully-feeling world, we would never need to wonder about what others might do or think since we would know that they too are merely responding to their feelings as are we. Then it would become obvious just how repressive current cultural norms are. There are always, in every culture (and group), those who are different and wish to go against the expected norms of their group. This tendency demonstrates that a cultural group is not as monolithic as we might have presumed. Furthermore, I feel it demonstrates that we hang on to our cultural heritages only at times when the supposed society (culture) we belong to seems threatened. I contend our cultural heritage is often portrayed as something it is not.

From within any cultural group, there are many factions and these often take on the same characteristics we use in defending the greater community at large. I feel that we intrinsically are individuals first and we only band together in the event of a presumed threat from the outside. If any group feels threatened, is this not what might in fact incite an actual threat—a self-fulfilling prophecy? Is this what is happening in the world currently?

It is very easily conceivable that even another group of individuals has quite different and perhaps opposing notions, but we do not have to turn them into conflicts.

Can anthropology give us any clues as to how neurosis started? Perhaps. Bernard Campbell, an anthropology professor at Cambridge University, England, made this proposition: As the human population increased in Africa, many started migrating north and eventually crossed over into Europe that was far colder than Africa (especially central Africa) where we humans perhaps started. In Europe shelter was only readily available in caves. The problem with communal living in caves was that crying babies became an imposition on the rest of the cave community requiring some authoritarian leaders to make decisions in order to make life a little more bearable for these new cave-dwellers. These authorities now started to impose rules.

This is only speculation from an anthropologist. Only something similar could have instigated the growth of neurosis. If Europe is where neurosis was born, it is not too far fetched to see that this also was the birth of Western civilization. I will leave it to future anthropologists to conjecture about other possible ways.

Having talked about culture in part II, I suggest that we do not need culture since most cultural heritages stem from our earlier notions of what was needed to keep our original smaller communities in some sort of order. This relates directly to what I said of Marvin Harris' book *Cows, Pigs, Wars and Witches* where he suggested most of our rights and rituals were mundane economic factors in deciding how that culture (society) might benefit. Our earlier tribal leaders were not able to express it in economic terms since we were too primitive in our thinking then—as I mentioned earlier, a connection between thinking and language. A friend of mine studying linguistics and etymology suggests non-literate societies do not think in the abstract. Before the written word, perhaps there was little by way of concepts (thinking in the abstract).

Cultural development

As societies grew larger and travel was made easier as was also the absorption of small groups into larger groups, there developed a binding together of all of the original smaller group rights and rituals into more and more complex cultural norms.

As we became more sophisticated in our religious notions and adapted to more modern social and economic necessities, then both our religious and cultural ideas became more complex; at this stage, we needed to set up a culture with laws, initially based on the necessities of a ruling class to maintain leadership and get the populace at large to comply. The political evolution led to more and more sophistication through what we now deem law justifying it by order, hence 'law and order' which suggest if there was no law, there would automatically be no order—not a logical given, depending on what we consider constitutes order.

Differing cultures evolve from their own histories which is why we get conflicts of interest from one culture with another. This is the current dilemma with the so-called "Middle East crisis": the major culture's (Western civilization) notion that our's is the one culture we should all want to emulate, is only held by that dominant culture which ignores its own as well as others' histories.

I contend that all cultures are our worst enemies and now fail to serve (as Marvin Harris implies), for we are caught up in our own cultural histories. We need to contemplate abolishing our preconceived notions of culture and its necessity and start to see it as a hindrance to both our moral and economic needs, especially if we are to compare the economics of value (money) with the economics of desire. If we could make this conceptual leap, we might well see our way to a cooperative way of being rather than our current competitive one. We have presumed that culture is noble and beautiful. I suggest that culture is a hindrance to a global means for us to coexist on this planet peacefully and cooperatively.

Culture and sex

Our cultural habits encroach upon our well-being also in the area of love and sex. We little understand our sexualities, let alone our ability to love in the many ways and means we have at our disposal. A case in point might be homosexuals who need to create their own circumstances about their own lives. No one would be telling them that this or that was immoral, wrong or disgusting and as this degree of independence gets transposed to each of us individually, our desires will begin to seem "natural" (whatever "natural" is supposed to mean). My next chapter deals first with our cultural concepts of sexuality and our cultural inhibitions. Our natural individual means of expressing sexuality, as opposed to our cultural notion that sex is only for procreation.

23

Sex and Love

in a non-neurotic world

What we have considered sexually "normal" in our neurotic cultures has been nothing more than the average. There is craziness in this analysis since all of us, one way or another, have our sexual deviations, but many will deny this. In this sense, there is no such thing as average or even, for that matter, majority deviance. In our neurotic world, most of us are reluctant to talk about sex, let alone admit to our deviances (except perhaps with others with the near same deviance). All of us are different and for a good reason, because if we were not, we would be going after the very same sex partner.

Without the early traumas that bring about sexual perversions and inversions, only then might we, in an abstract way, suggest we are "normal." What I described as the addictive nature of sex and the perverted sexual practices would not exist because, ostensibly, there would be no need to kill old pain. Then we would all just pursue our own unique desires to express ourselves sexually. I contend that would only be through love.

The question I do not have an answer to is: Would we then still desire sex and yet have little or no feeling of affection (love) for the person we were indulging in sex with? Unless both parties were on the same wavelength, I doubt that could ever take place. I feel young children might indulge in just playful sex as their early expressions of their sexuality and experiments with one another.

Development of sexuality

Sex and our sexuality are probably where we manifest neurosis mostly. I am not sure if there exist cultures that allow one the freedom to express sexuality simply and naturally from birth to death. I say from birth meaning that at birth our sexuality at best is very primitive and basic if it exists at all.

Most cultures seem not to accept that from birth (maybe actually conception) onwards, we are developing our sexuality until it reaches maturity. It is questionable as to when sexual maturity is achieved, but we need to permit the natural experiences of sexuality from its basic instincts just as we permit the natural experiences of most of our other developments. Just as we grow physically and mentally, so also do we grow sexually. It's not necessarily smooth and does have moments of heightened acceleration. The crazy notion that one day we are totally asexual and the next day suddenly sexually mature and knowledgeable and experienced is absurd in the extreme. Where and when are we supposed to get our knowledge and experience from? I know no one who at an early age in childhood did not have some sexual feelings from time to time, even if at that stage they felt guilty because it was considered wrong. When and where are those notions planted? I contend that it is in all cultural moralities. The idea that one's sexual organs and sensations in those organs are immoral, wrong and dirty is simply neurotic.

In the Judeo-Christian tradition, the scriptural teachings of Judaism from the Old Testament (Leviticus and Deuteronomy) and then the preachings of Saul of Tarsus (St. Paul) are the most restrictive of sexual expression leaving Christianity and Judaism (perhaps Islam also) with the legacy today culminating in the stupidity of "Just say no." I contend that inhibiting our natural growth and development in our sexual expression is precisely what causes the later problems of our sexual practices from the perversions to the unwanted pregnancies, adultery, divorce and sexual addiction causing overpopulation that now plagues the human race.

Even more absurd is the amount of subliminal sexuality in everyday capitalist life with such things as advertising, the way we dress and also in our entertainment, especially sport. This must affect children very profoundly and causes all the complexities of adolescence in both sexes. I wonder how the Christian Right is able to account for the enormous amount of pornography among so called "normal" people and the billions spent on it and, *I suspect*, among the very Christian Right practitioners.

The designation of the various sexual orientations (heterosexuality, homosexuality, bisexuality, transsexualism) is something only neurotics have devised. Designation of righteousness or wrongteousness to these acts is something of a 'puzzlement', for it serves no real or societal purpose for us. In the early days of neurosis among us humans, I can only assume that procreation was so vital to the species that somehow we needed to punish those that did not actively contribute. Sadly, we imposed our will through morality and that marked the beginnings of religious thoughts and notions. From early childhood we have been very aware of love, particularly for our parents, but there was never any sexuality (from the child) in the early stages of this kind of love. The sensuality of touch and caressing was surely all there and the pleasure and comfort enormous, but it never, as far as I can tell, created any sensuality in the genitals. In those cases where an adult might get sexual satisfaction with their child, I contend that it was the neurosis of the adult confusing sensuality with sexuality, sensuality being the stimulations of the senses, as opposed to sexuality being the stimulation of the sexual organs.

Love

I don't know if it applies to most languages, but the word love in English has many meanings, from the love of inanimate objects and pastimes to the deepest feelings when we use the phrase "fallen in love." Our use of the word "love" is actually very ambiguous and can range form love of the outdoor life all the way to romantic love of another human with whom we would want to include sex. I find it unfortunate that we use this one word in its generic sense for all these different kinds of love. I feel that in a nonneurotic (feeling-full) world, we would invent some differentiation. I feel very strongly that the neurotic's generalized use of this word rationalizes, in the mind of those neurotics that desire sex with children or animals, that their so-called love justifies their desire for gratification from that kind of sex. Sadly, this is not the driving force for their desire, merely their (often very sincere) justification of that desire. I do not see sex outside the context of romantic love as being feeling-full.

Relationships

Real love for another living creature is a two-way process, better described as a relationship: a state of being related, having a connectedness. Other than blood, the connectedness between humans having a relationship is no more than a feeling-flow between them. I would, for the most part, include one's relationships with other creatures, especially pets. Relationships with inanimate objects or desires are really attitudes towards those objects and would be better defined as "attitudes" rather than "relationships."

Janov defined real love between humans as "permitting the loved one to be exactly who they are," something we neurotics are unable to permit because, I contend, that was not what happened for all of us in our childhoods. Hence real love eludes most of us.

So where would the place of sex be in a non-neurotic (feeling-full) world? Again, the best we can do is only conjecture. I will make mine bearing in mind that I could well be wrong, but hope that my conjecture will inspire others to make theirs from the perspective of an understanding of Primal Theory and a general sense of a non-neurotic world.

The ultimate sexual gratification would come only from real romantic love with another appropriate and compatible human that was reciprocating it. "Lovers" is the word that I would use for such a relationship. I would exclude that word from any other kind of relationship.

24

Relearning

learning in a non-neurotic world

I feel we have some idea of the effects with respect to education in view of the experiment at Summerhill and other "free schools" around the world. Children and students would makes decisions as to when and where to learn, what it was interested in and the instructors at these facilities would have to make it interesting to their students, otherwise the pupils would leave and go elsewhere. I am convinced wanting something to do rather than curiosity would drive their motives in a direct manner. The child makes its own decisions as to what it desires and wants to know and on what time frame to accomplish those goals.

Just how much we would want or need to learn can only be left to conjecture, but I am certain that a lot of the extraneous stuff we are compelled to learn in our present-day schools would become irrelevant. I do feel that what we need to learn most is how to live with one another, both in the smaller and larger communities and then as a global community—a learning process, but not a teachable one. As we progressed, the need to let all our learning take place and evolve in its own good way would become clear.

This relatively simple concept has eluded us: left alone, most of us, especially children, would find their own niche for whatever they considered was right for them. They would have the luxury at any stage to change their minds and pursue any other avenue they liked. This would continue for as long as they deemed it necessary.

Letting others do as they wish (desire) is not necessarily an imposition on the rest of us. If it disrespects our moral bounds, then we need to look to our morality—something within us. Otherwise, all that we need to do is to react appropriately (emotionally) to that person and permit them to counter-react. This notion is alien to our current neurotic responses. What we currently do creates conflict—an unlikely inspiration for cooperative living.

The learning process

Since we learn a great deal long before we go into any formal education system, this could eventually continue without schools as we know them today. Maybe there would just be people that children would gravitate towards (parents at first, then later others like family members, then neighbors) who would answer children's questions and perhaps suggest tasks to help them understand their curiosities, desires and interests. Perhaps the notion currently called schools would cease to exist or be necessary. What would become obvious is that our current system of authority from above would gradually evaporate and that children would truly be in the position to show us adults just what direction we should be gravitating towards. This is another hard concept for us to accept at this juncture.

It is only when we start down this route that certain directions will become obvious and, as each generation follows, we will see more clearly what we collectively need to know and learn. That is why I suggest that we cannot in any way predict how any of this might turn out. The best we might do for the moment is to merely conjecture, but be ready and willing to adapt as time progresses. Initially, we must recognize the need to allow learning and abandon the top-down approach of being taught and all the concomitant thinking and decisions that follow this approach.

To educate

We use the notion of "to educate" in many spheres of our lives and contend that we can solve many of the problems that we collectively encounter by educating others. Homosexuals, for example, presume that an understanding (education) of their situation and predicament can be taught. Cultural conflict assumes that if only one could educate the opposition, then we might resolve the conflict. Politics offers the same remedy. Without feeling-fullness there is *no* real understanding.

Punishment is not and never will be a teaching process; it actually facilitates the reverse—hence the madness of incarceration. Only when we are able to fully-feel will we recognize and empathize how it might be for others. In this sense education has grossly failed. We need to relearn the means and rationale of feelings, something we were actually born with, but then lost. If children were allowed to retain their sense of feelings, then little by way of education (teaching) would be necessary to live a full-quality life that comes only from being able to experience our being (to feel it).

The steps

I initially called this chapter reeducation but quickly realized that it was a relearning process. I contend the steps in this relearning process are actually quite simple in concept though I concede that persevering to achieve that goal is very complicated and difficult because we believed so much of this extraneous learning was absolutely necessary in the first place. To make this conceptual leap necessitates that we acknowledge that our current path is leading us into disaster. Subliminally, most of us know that the current state of affairs is on a wrong path, but there is little by way of ideas as to what is the right path. Alcoholics in their twelve-step programs need to first acknowledge that they have a problem within themselves. Just admitting to the problem—"I am an alcoholic"—suggests being halfway to resolving it. I concur with that. We need to do the same with neurosis. Acknowledging our neurosis is halfway to resolving it.

25

Cooperation, not Competition

It was early in the 19th century that the idea of cooperation came to life in the Western world and was, in the early days, used to create a retail store that would collectively buy wholesale and resell to its members who would reap dividends relative to what each member spent. Further experiments have been carried out with employee suggestion boxes and how the company might benefit from those ideas coming up from the bottom. Now we see some employee-owned companies flourishing, some in Argentine as well as here in the United States. The ones in Argentine are apperntly very democratically operated. It is not yet generally acceptable to run things from the bottom up as we have for far too long presumed a top-down exigency, but it is rapidly becoming evident that "top-down" is not now productive.

As stated in Chapter 19, cooperation works best in organizations where most of the workers are volunteers. Authoritarianism becomes mute under these circumstances and is replaced by suggestions and countersuggestions and ultimately the group deciding on the best compromise after considering all ideas. We might easily conceive running the whole world cooperatively, from the bottom up, not the top-down as we have been doing for millennia.

We need to reverse this ever-growing expansion of the corporate world of business. It is erroneously assumed that market forces are a simple concept that levels the playing field and brings about some natural order. This is the greatest nuerotic myth of all time. It is the credo of right wing politics of all stripes that perpetuates this ritualistic myth. We are begining to see now this too does not work. It has moved away from personal contact with employees to a less feeling-full authoritarian system. It created a division of labor that made the whole enterprise cumbersome and discouraged a great deal of the enthusiasm. As an example, we see the results of all this now with the United States government allotting contracts to major corporations for reconstruction in Iraq. This is privatization gone mad and wasteful not only monetarily, but also in lives and livelihoods except for those at the top of the management chain. It also creates the power structure for corporations that is rapidly becoming bigger than governments and will consume us all within its neurotic (unfeelingful) notions.

Corporate madness

Just as politically-conservative purists feel that government is too large and cumbersome and the bureaucracies required to run and organize things are way out of control, so also, I contend, big business and corporations manifest the very same problems. As any small organization knows well, as the organization expands, so do the internal mechanisms that keep it efficient. The only way out of this dilemma is to break down the whole process right to the very base level of the individual and permit bottom-up cooperation. There is a problem if workers are coerced into having to do work "in order that"—no matter what "that" reason is.

We found a way around this in the early part of the nineteenth century with the formation of the labor unions which initially were democratic, but later also became larger and larger so they too encountered the very same bureaucratic hierarchy. Again, we have realized that the smaller the unit, the better control it would have over itself.

Marxism

Marx assumed one way to prevent the cumbersome nature of government was through the trade union principle that would establish control from the bottom up. Alas, with the Russian experiment, (Stalin in particular) the labor union became subservient to the hierarchy of government, which in turn set out to protect itself from the so-called masses that (it said) could not be trusted.

Until and unless we can break it all down to the very sovereignty of the individual and see the very nature of cooperation, we are never going to overcome the nagging concept that most neurotics take for granted: "the need to be controlled."—*not me ... but the other guy*

This to me is the great tragedy of our time. The very essence of fully feeling is to relinquish control of others on all levels, from the personal to the family, to the larger family unit, to the community, to the society in general and then, unto the whole world, but most of all to the human world community.   That is why policing, prison wardens, militarism, and criminal justice syetems are redundant, expensive and further compound neurosis. In the end resolve nothing for the community or us humans individualy.

The underpinnings of the subconcious.

We are subconsciously afraid. We are subconsciously angry. We are subconsciously sad. These subconscious feelings are running us. We neurotics are all of these to some extent or other. I feel that one of them for each of us predominate the other two. Whichever one dominates will be the deciding factor in how we think, how we act and how we behave, commonly referred to as our personalities. We believe these feelings are in and created by the present when in fact they most often belong to our past, but we have no connection to them. Our ideas and ideations get wrapped within this fallacy which leads to a whole host of assumptions about the only way we can be. Just by simply acknowledging the subconscious and knowing that it contains only past pain, might we slowly begin to see an alternative way to conduct life for ourselves on this very, very beautiful planet … before we destroy it.

We do not need to be cooperative with everyone we encounter, however; we do not need to compete with them either. We can just leave them alone—live and let live.

26

Art, Science and Medicine

in a non-neurotic world

Art

I contend that everyday life would stimulate feelings and we would accept this natural stimulation of all the things around us, even if the outcome was not necessarily to our liking. Art would take on a completely new meaning and the potential for all to be artists from time to time would abound. Some would be comedians to make us laugh; others would stir us to awe and surprise. The fun in life would be much more prevalent. Of course, moments of grief and sadness would still be present, like the death of a friend or loved one. Also, there would still be things to fear such as natural disasters, but we would be far more able to accept them than we do now.

Science

The desire for scientific endeavours would be left to those with a real curiosity to doodle in scientific pursuits. Scientists in a non-neurotic world would never want to invent or create some horror like a nuclear bomb or military armaments, especially landmines and cluster bombs to blow the limbs off children—sick weapons if ever there were any. Guns and bullets also would be seen for what they are—killing tools. They would be very reserved about creating something that in the future could jeopardize our existence such as fuels that create global warming and eventually compromise life for us all. Scientists, in order to do their experimenting, would need to garner cooperation to interest others in their specialized pursuits. If these experiments needed colossal endeavors like outer-space explorations or huge atom-smasher circuits, they would first need to find a large-enough groups of people wanting and desiring these same experiments—again, the economics of desire. One area where especially scientific endeavor might be utilized could be in limiting the amount of energy needed (especially in the first world) to maintain comfort and mobility—do we really need to run around in two-ton automobiles for mobility?

Medicine

In the field of medicine, we would pursue prevention and not spend time on cures, which, I repeat, is like "trying to close the barn door when the horse has bolted." I further contend that we would be saved from many current diseases as the outcome of early pain relegated into the subconscious. I contend most diseases are the outcome of a lifetime of old feelings reverberating in the subconscious, seeking to escape (to be expressed). Even accidents would be less prevalent.

In a non-neurotic world, the desire for art, science and medicine, as we currently understand them, would be drastically changed. I can only conjecture or perhaps persuade others to conjecture on their own.

Where did all the excitement go?

In order to understand our need to be emotionally stimulated, we ought to take a look at what we do now to that end. The number of digressions we seek is enormous, from entertainment to the various addictive pursuits. Most of it is mere diversion and rarely ever really exciting. We neurotics seem to be relatively content if we can just get by on a day-to-day basis and, for the most part, we seem unable to accomplish much by way of contentment. I remember many years ago when a friend remarked: "Life's a bitch and then you die." It came as something of a shock to me and I wanted to immediately protest, but on thinking about it, realized it was true and that there was indeed very little to get excited about unlike when I was quite young. Where did all that excitement go? Why can't we still have it? Falling in love used to be so thrilling. Why can't we still fall so gloriously in love or be so excited about simple things? Why is our entertainment (especially TV) so dull and lacking in exhilaration? Maybe only sport offers us this kind of thrill, even though it's often at the expense of the other competitor. Of course, there remain the perverse thrills dreamed up by serious neurotics, most especially TV and film violence. Sex, for sure, offers another, at least for some of us.

Doodling in scientific pursuits would not be that prevalent either. The eagerness to enroll in a profession of scientific investigation among feeling-full people would lose most of its glamour and all of its prestige. It would just be a simple desire for those few so inclined. Certainly what one might want to doodle in would be contingent upon others who were equally willing to pursue a similar venture. One could get caught up in others' enthusiasm, but not necessarily for a great amount of time. I contend that scientific ventures would be more small-scale rather than the larger ones like outer-space projects. Outer-space exploration would have little or no interest and wanting to know the nature of the universe or its beginnings would hold much less interest for non-neurotics. A great deal of enthusiasm would be needed for those interested in such ventures. Those people would be left to their own devices or, in the case of large projects, there would be a need to gather many participants in those ventures which, like water, would find their very own level.

The medical profession

In the area of medicine, there might be more inclination to seek ways to alleviate suffering, which would not necessarily vanish. I contend there would be far fewer diseases and in particular those diseases resulting from neurosis. Malaria and insect-borne diseases might need some research for relief. Most of this could be relatively simple. In such areas as HIV, we already know how to prevent the epidemic spread of this virus and it would not be too far into the future that we might further prevent the spread, even if we were not able to come up with a cure. I have this infection, but fortunately am able to take medication and have relatively good health. We already have a good angle on the prevention of many other diseases like T.B. It's not that we need to preserve all life at all costs. There would inevitably be accidents and unfortunate infections and premature deaths, but I feel very strongly that most of these would be seen clearly as "the gamble of life" without that gamble having to necessitate belonging to a privileged sect.

Summary

Though art (the artificial stimulation of feelings), science (the insatiable desire to know about everything) and medicine (the search and need to cure all) are prevalent in this neurotic world. I feel, in a feeling-full world, these would greatly change.

27

Without Law, Government and Money

We could carry the idea of cooperation through to all areas of life and living. There would be no need of incentives to coerce people into doing work. The only incentives required would be simple, innate desires.

Some years ago, I encountered a situation where people were throwing litter in the street right outside my garden gate. I hated this litter so badly that one day I decided to spend the first 20 minutes after breakfast cleaning it up for my own satisfaction. My boyfriend at the time was incensed that I would do this "filthy job." I persisted in doing it every morning and over a period of time I began to notice that there was less litter in the street. This impelled me to go further and I started to do a little weeding up and down the street. Within a six-month period, it became the cleanest street in the block. It was not some complicated notion that encouraged me to do this but a simple desire to live in a clean street—the economy of desire. This notion carried to its extreme would produce a general sense that each of us, in any given community, would be willing to perform relatively easy tasks each individual was able to carry out and deemed desirable.

No one would need to work to get food, pay the rent or keep warm (or cool). I feel, in order to prevent boredom, we would all take on tasks. Those tasks that needed more than one person would garner other people who would cooperate to perform those things that the community at large needed for comfortable survival.

So how do we get from our current capitalist system to a system of total cooperation (anarchy)? Marxist communism was one idea which I believe was deliberately thwarted by the capitalist nations of the world. It was a great pity and I feel that Stalin, who took over from Lenin, realized that the "capitalist West" was bent on destroying their revolution and he became a tyrant in order to prevent its destruction. Alas, his tyranny eventually destroyed the revolution from within. If we could see it was neurosis that destroyed that attempt, we would have a better understanding of it and perhaps a better idea how to realize a revolution of our own. No one would need to labor for more than maybe 2 or 3 hours a day. The amount of energy that goes into collecting money could be better used for other purposes.

A new way of conceiving it

The conceptual leap needed to embrace what I am suggesting is a major one, but I hope some readers who have now begun to understand Primal Theory and see the ease of cooperation, might be willing to give it some thought. However, in the meantime, I will suggest some ways to maybe reach a position where we might start to live cooperatively. A few people (a critical mass) might hopefully begin to contemplate it and formulate discussion which will stimulate others to propose their own ideas.

We do have some precedent for this that I will expound upon. Both Copernicus and Galileo were ostracized for their then-outrageous idea that the earth was not the center of the universe. So preposterous was his notion considered to be that Galileo was excommunicated and greatly punished. Eventually the concept was accepted, inspite of the chruch and and but for a few "Flat Earth Society" people, universally accepted. Could it be that in the near future we might be able to accept the implications of Primal Theory and cooperative anarchy? I firmly hope and believe it will be so. Meanwhile, here are some ways we might progress towards a non-neurotic way of life.

How might we move towards a feeling-full system?

The Dissenters of London, in the late seventeenth century, were apparently the very first anarchists. This was a group of people who moved out to some common land to try an experiment of cooperation with other like-minded people to work with what I earlier called the economy of desire. They were never allowed to flourish and were dispersed by the current ruling authority. We might still be able to emulate their example. The experiment would certainly need not to be interfered with and perhaps initially protected with some outside assistance. If not, then the problem becomes: How do we get from our current capitalist system to a system of total cooperation (anarchy)?

There have been other attempts and one notable one was during the Spanish civil war when the people of Catalonia (the area around Barcelona) established an almost pure anarchistic system. Sadly, this was also thwarted by General Franco who marched in and destroyed it. How it might have fared had it been allowed to flourish is anyone's guess, but when I lived in Ibiza (one of the Balearic Islands off the east coast of Spain and part of Catalonia) during the 1970s, I met and talked to many local people who remained adamant anarchists. Maybe not in the full intellectual sense of that word, but they knew in their hearts that they did not need government and law.

Many political thinkers have thought through this same idea over time including Pierre-Joseph Prudhon, the French anarchist, and later the Russians Mikhail Bakunin and then Peter Kropotkin. However, the most famous of anarchistic thinkers was Karl Marx along with Friedrich Engels. What Marx did was try to create a system whereby we might transition from a capitalist system (as he coined it) to a full anarchistic way of life for all on the planet. In the meantime, Marx and his ideas have been trashed and dismissed because the Russian experiment never got beyond socialist capitalism. The withering away of the state was never contemplated, let alone tried.

Awareness of Primal Theory

Had there been an understanding of neurotic acting out, the communist revolution could have actually succeeded. However, the West's determination to thwart the socialism of this new state did encourage the Soviets to create a military that could prevent its destruction from outside. It almost succeeded except for the elite nature of the politburo whose secrecy and paranoia deemed it necessary to force a consensus from the population. Had there been a stricter adherence to Marx by allowing the unions to politicize from the bottom up, I feel there would have been a very different outcome and a more feeling-full one. Could a current communist state attempt this transition? If so, I feel it would need to be one of the smaller ones. What comes to my mind is Cuba, the nemesis of the United States.

Is there the possibility that we could initiate a process to evolve from our present capitalist system into a full-cooperative and feeling-full system that did not need the symbols of money as a means of control, or laws that endeavored to control it? I say yes, based on the Barcelona experiment mentioned above and reflecting back to the Summerhill school notion under A. S. Neill whereby we let the children/people decide how and when and in what way they need to be educated/socialized. Permit a political system from the bottom up as opposed to the system of so-called representational democracy we currently have—from the top-down.

Maybe we could try it out in small communities or perhaps small companies so that the people in these situations made the decisions which got carried on up through the hierarchy. Then groups of communities or businesses could in turn use representatives from the smaller groups to manage and decide how to conduct business or run their now-larger communities. In turn, these collaborative larger units would send representatives to even larger groups which in turn would be beholden only to the underlying groups. This would go on unto even larger groups and on up until we eventually had representatives on a so-called national level and thence continue further still until we had an international set of representatives implementing factors for the greater good of the world community as a whole. However, the lower community would need to control the representatives sent to the higher levels with immediate replacement if they failed in their true representation, preventing the corrupting effects on representatives once installed, which is the current state of affairs.

First we might try by taking the money out of politics simply by making lobbying of politicians as well as political campaign contributions non-tax-deductible. Overturn the ruling and notion that money is speech—a neurotic notion if ever there was one. Permit free access in all public communications to any and all contenders for political office. Make all ballots proportional representation, allowing for easier access by third-party contenders without them necessarily being spoilers.

Encourage volunteerism. There are many ideas for promoting this from a two-year conscription process for youth desiring further education to retirees wanting to do something useful and exhilarating in retirement. Once the process was started, I feel sure that others, having most of their general needs met, would eagerly follow. This trend among some people would in turn generate a greater spirit among more of the people until there was general acceptance—an evolutionary process. However, it would require the populous to lead in all this as the Politians are way too spineless and corrupt to engender *any* of it.

28

Childrearing

merely a suggestion for a non-neurotic world

In order to transition from our current neurotic state, we need to completely rethink our current childrearing practices. Therefore, to me, this is perhaps the most important chapter; however, I hesitate a lot to even make any suggestion here since I have never brought a child into this world, let alone reared one. My only authority is that I was once a child so this is from a child's perspective, not a parent's. Since I do not know any parent that succeeded in rearing a non-neurotic child, I feel that parental experience counts for very little. It could be said that I have no ideas about the difficulties, but I contend that 99% of the difficulties with childrearing are due to traumatizing the child (inadvertently perhaps) and not the upbringing per se.

We need to accept that children, even newborns, are sovereign unto themselves. The child's fully-feeling self will respond appropriately to get its needs met and a fully-feeling parent will know instinctively what the child needs. As the child progressed in life, it would become easier and easier on parents to just allow the child to decide what it needed and wanted and understand the difference between *need* and *want*, however, this necessitates fully-feeling parents.

What could be done to let the child be itself when the current parent is still neurotic? This is a question that many who have done Primal Therapy for an extended period of time find difficult to answer. There is no "how to" that I can tell anyone, nor is there anyone I know of who can give a "how to." I will proffer one suggestion—as best you can, attempt at all times (especially in the first year) to stay with and figure out what the child is asking for, using your own feelings.

There are several books that I feel would be helpful and the first relates to the very birthing process: *Birth Without Violence* by Dr. Frederick LeBoyer, a French obstetrician. Another is *The Continuum Concept* by Jean Leidloff who studied childrearing practices among the indigenous tribes of the Andes. Also, there is a book where a father brought up his own son after he divorced: *Real Fatherhood* by Bob Kamm. I cried reading this book, seeing that his child, Benjamin, (affectionately called Bengi-bo), got much of what I wanted, but never fully got. Then there is an Australian documentary of some experiments with newborns called *Kangaroo Mother Care*. Each of these suggests new ways of taking care of our young and the way we might look at childrearing. Lastly, we need to look seriously into circumcision of male babies (a barbaric act if ever there was one) and caesarian section birthing.

I suggest that a crying baby is a baby in pain, period. If the child is crying, it needs to be held until the caregiver (mother) can ascertain what it is that the child needs. There are very few possibilities after all other needs have been met. Needing to be fed, needing to be cleaned, needing to be kept warm, needing to feel safe, needing to breathe freely, and needing to be held. I contend that any mother having gone through nine months of pregnancy has many instinctive abilities to feel what the child currently needs. As the child develops, assuming that all prior needs are met, it becomes relatively easy for the caregivers to know what is required. By the time the child has words and gestures and can crawl, I contend discovering what the child needs becomes easier and easier to ascertain, considering that it was always possible to acquiesce to those needs socially. The one requisite is that the caregivers (parents) love and want that child from the outset.

If the mother is the primary caregiver, then the father needs to be totally supportive of that mother and child without expecting anything in return for his effort. Mothering is total and leaves little or no time for that twosome which evaporated the minute there was a child on the way. We need to dispense with the myth that creating a child enhances the twosome nature of the original relationship. It becomes, by definition, a threesome at least. In our current neurotic world, it takes 26 hours a day for both partners to bring up just one child. Yes, that means it can never be fully achieved in our current civilization.

It is on these grounds, if the mother (or couple) did not want the child, then an abortion ought always to be allowable. Being unwanted creates a trauma to the fetus that continues after birth. If the newborn is fostered off or adopted, it creates further trauma and the beginnings of neurosis which even the most skilled and aware caregiver would find almost impossible to negate or reverse.

The prerequisite

The prerequisite for wanting a child ought to be only that both partners (potential parents) want that child for its own sake. Sadly, there are many reasons couples and indiviuals have for wanting a child other than what I just stated. The egotistical one of desiring to reproduce ourselves is perhaps the worst based on the false notion that it is a natural desire. Much of this is promoted through religious notions. Another is the common belief that having a child will enhance the relationship. Chances are greater it will do the opposite or at least make the relationship more difficult. A twosome relationship at the onset of pregnancy becomes (I repeat) immediately a threesome (presuming that there was no other child so far). Twosomes are complicated enough without the added complication of a third human being. Further additions will complicate matters even more. However, if both parents really want a child or children for their own sake, then they give them a great start in life. If one or the other partner does not want the child, then going ahead with the pregnancy is invariably catastrophic for that child and potentially for the relationship as well. It is suggested that abortion is killing. I agree in principle, but there is killing and killing. Sadly, we are left with the legacy of "Thou shalt not kill." Is killing a pesky fly or accidentally walking on and killing some colony of ants crossing our path considered a sin in the eyes of God? Are a few thousands cells in a uterus any more sacrosanct than a colony of ants or a pesky fly? It appears hypocritical to me that killing a fully-grown human in war or through the criminal justice system seems not to cause much of a stir, yet paradoxically antiabortionists insist on saving a few thousand cells in the uterus based, *presumably*, on the same God-given commandment.

Birth without violence

Dr. Frederick LeBoyer in his book *Birth Without Violence* suggested that current obstetric practices are in many instances violent. Since his publication, there seems to have been some movement towards making the birthing process less painful for the child and there have been studies done to show that this does indeed benefit the child in its later development, which should be obvious. There have been several other publications also pointing this out but are too numerous for me to recount here. Janov points this out in great detail in all of his books, particularly his latest, *Primal Healing*. I suggest reading Janov will further elaborate on this.

Kangaroo mother care

Some months ago I saw a recorded documentary from an Australian television company called *Kangaroo Mother Care* which moved me. It was attempting to demonstrate that maybe we humans as upright beings actually produced a situation in the gestation process whereby the fetus needed to be born before completion of that gestation. If correct, the notion, based on the fact that most other creatures are able to stand within minutes of their birth, might corroborate this hypothesis. Human babies are unable to do this and it takes a year after birth just to walk. The exception are the marsupials who have this very convenient pouch for the young to climb into after birth to stay and be nurtured and fed with little extra attention from the mother. The program showed how some obstetricians in Australia experimented with newborns letting them seek the breasts of the mother and from thereon be physically carried by the mother in what they cited as an extension of the gestation period. This offered the newborns the safety of being next to the mother's skin for an extended period of another 9 months. The babies were easily fed and kept warm and could reach the breast at the time they (the baby) needed to be fed. Also, the mother became acutely aware of when her offspring needed to defecate and be cleaned. It also suggested that the mother and child needed to sleep together for at least this extended gestation. We don't have the natural pouch, but it is a very easy matter to have a sling around the mother's neck and side to facilitate the carrying. It further suggests that perambulators for babies are not the way to go. Babies feel safer when they are in physical contact with the mother. I remember this well as a baby myself. It was unbelievable how safe I felt next to my "mammy" and how scary when not in physical contact.

Circumcision

Only neurotics could think up a practice as barbaric and stupifyingly unnatural as removing the foreskin of males' penises. To suggest it is cleaner and easier to manage in childhood and adulthood is absurd. I know from my younger days with other boys that the only ones that had difficulty with their penises were the ones that were never allowed to play with them. Boys playing with their penises and pulling the foreskin back is natural and normal. It is neurotic parents that inculcate a "no-no" unto their children playing with their genitals. Cultural traditions in this regard demonstrate the absurdity.

Caesarian Section

Initially this was a practice reserved only for emergencies when the mother or child's life was threatened by a normal birth. Now it seems three other factors have crept into play: first, doctors' concerns about a malpractice suit unless they perform a caesarian birth rather than risk a difficult outcome; second, the greater convenience for the obstetricians' working hours; third, some mothers may be concerned about stretching the vagina. This unnatural surgery has an enormous impact on the "to-be-born." Several primal patients, reliving their own caesarian birth, have noted that it leaves them with a sense of never completing. I contend further that a woman who underwent a caesarian birth herself must be unprepared to deal with birthing her own child and it suggests that this practice should never be undertaken except in the most extreme circumstances.

Boundaries

On the question of creating boundaries for children, I contend this is another of our neurotic, tragic myths. If parents can respond to the actions and reactions of a child through their own emotional responses (without threatening the child in any way), I feel the child will readily accept and accommodate instinctively towards the parental emotions (expressions). Just as the child needs the freedom to express itself, so do the caregivers need to express their own feelings appropriately also. The child is born into an environment with the caregivers (normally mother and father). If this is a fully-feeling environment, nothing more would ever be needed. If the child's needs are met, then its desires and wants will naturally be adaptable and there is no need to create "boundaries." The child will adapt to the feelings of its environment naturally (I am not talking here of preventing danger, but even in this regard reacting to their (the parents') feelings is the aim. See *Continuum Concept* by Jean Liedloff. All this is easier said than done, in particular if the caregiver is neurotic. Neurotics operate from act-outs and non-feeling-full responses always confuse the child. I am certain that if the caregiver responds appropriately to their own feelings, the child will accept this. When I say appropriate responses, I mean ones that are expressed directly and not as a threat or demand upon the child. This is tricky to actually describe, but in a primal context, I feel, makes a lot of sense. I will try in the next paragraph to give some examples, but these too must not be taken literally but in their context and the reader needs to think this through. Thinking out a game plan for boundaries is crazy. It needs to come from one's instincts and feelings, not principles. Neurotics think and act in terms of principles; sadly, they have little or no other means.

Delineating the appropriate feeling responses to children

Guidelines are easy to give, but are almost impossible to carry out. Nevertheless, I will state them. If the caregiver will express her feelings about what it is the child is doing without physically hurting (threatening) the child, without *dumping* on the child, it will be able to feel that response and, I contend, accept it without being in any way traumatized, and having to repress pain. As I stated earlier, frustrations to a child are not traumatic or harmful and the child can easily adjust to them. Trauma comes with overwhelming feelings that the child is unable to integrate unto itself. The child is naturally feeling-full provided that all prior needs have been met. The catch phrase is *"all prior needs have been met."* If not, then we are already on a very difficult path in rearing the child and hoping to save it from neurosis. Even so, the fewer traumas, especially in the early part of life—first year—the less acting out will be needed by that child as it develops.

Old pain in babies

There is one other factor that I feel is not even vaguely understood by current childrearing practitioners, the medical profession or caregivers: we (as organisms) are forever attempting to bring the subconscious back into consciousness—healing ourselves. This starts to take place at the onset of feelings that are relegated into the subconscious. I contend that this occurs in babies and children that have already been traumatized and continues throughout life. This means if the child has enough sense of safety, it will self-primal, i.e. relive the older trauma. For caregivers, this must be very confusing as it seems there is absolutely no reason why the child is in pain (usually crying). If this were understood, it would require that the caregiver be able to stay with the child, holding it and giving it a sense of safety while it was able to relive its old pain with the caregivers allowing it to happen. Also, this might be a reoccurring event for the child until it was able to totally integrate that trauma. Only caregivers aware of the nature of reliving old pain (primaling) would be sensitive enough to allow this.

––––––––––

It would take more than just one book to go into childrearing in light of Primal Theory. Therefore, even though I feel this chapter is the most important one for establishing a non-neurotic society, by necessity it can only skirt this huge subject. I hope it might serve as an inspiration for others using Primal Theory. However, I also feel going into parenting should be no more than wanting that child for the *child's* sake—and not any other sake—with both parents prepared to give themselves totally to the child's needs (not wants). The necessity to read many books can exacerbate the situation rather than enlighten prospective parents, even though I have suggested a few titles.

Epilogue

Primal Therapy, I contend, will not save humanity or the planet. Primal Theory just might. Primal Theory is simple and easily understood. It explains all the factors about us humans that I have attempted to expound in this book. If, as I have suggested, Primal Theory is Unified Field Theory, then it surely does fall into that category of being simple and universally understandable.

Why did I call it a Gospel? I felt it was "the good word" that needed to be promulgated after experiencing my own therapy and knowing and undergoing the pain to relive it—if only it was possible to prevent this pain and suffering in the children of tomorrow.

I end this work relating my own progress in therapy over these 25 years, but before I do that, I would like to explain a few things about myself and my (neurotic) reasons for writing this book in the first place. When I first read *The Primal Scream*, I was so stricken with the book that I reread it immediately, just to make sure that I had gotten it right. I was at the time living in Ibiza, one of the Balearic Islands in the Mediterranean, with lots of other hippies. It was the Haight-Ashbury of Europe. I immediately tried to win over all my hippie friends and was devastated to discover that none were interested. Maybe it had to do with me and the way I was presenting it. In hindsight, I now know that unless one is near to some devastating old feelings, *The Primal Scream* seems somewhat dramatic in its claim. My need to proselytize was my own neurotic desire to be heard (an old pain of mine from childhood). I was not deterred and eventually was able to save enough to come to the United States in 1981 and started therapy soon thereafter.

It is an ongoing process and I have no doubt that I will have to continue to feel my old feelings, going deeper and deeper into my history. I actually, without knowing it, started therapy in that clinic in London. I knew after reading *The Primal Scream* that I wanted to do this therapy, not that I needed it. I was able early on to get into feelings of sadness about my childhood. It was not until later that I was able to get to some anger about what my father had done to me and my need for him. My therapy went quite well and I got into feelings very early relating mainly to my very strict father. After 18 months, I withdrew from formal therapy and worked with several buddies (fellow patients that "sit" for one another and listen in turn to one another). Then, some 5 years later, I was able to afford the yearly retreat that the Primal Institute ran each summer. I was really thrilled with the process at the retreats, an almost week-long residence program with 3-hour-long group sessions every day and other programs designed to promote feelings in a very beautiful setting, mainly in Montecito, Santa Barbara, California. I attended nearly all retreats from then on finding it very conducive to getting into my deeper feelings. I did decide some 4 years later to start to attend group sessions again and whenever I encountered a painful event in my life, would go and get some private sessions with a therapist all at the Primal Institute; meanwhile I was buddying (as we call it) with my buddies (I currently have 3) and progressing to earlier feelings in my childhood. I have had one primal about my birth and several feelings that have taken me back into the womb. These feelings are extremely devastating.

My life now feels relatively simple and I find I am able to listen, something I was hardly able to do before therapy. I am not nearly so nervous about many things and a lot of my twitching and neck twisting seems to have relaxed. I see other people's primal pain more easily which allows me to be more sympathetic towards them, and reduces my potential to be upset with the personality of others. Also, I see more clearly the reason for most things and hence feel less confused. The greatest attribute is: life is way more magical and way, way less mysterious. One other benefit is knowing why I am the way I am: the "good," the "bad" and the downright "ugly". One last point: it gave me the promise Arthur Janov claimed in *The Primal Scream* for me to become the real me.

Primal Theory is very simple and easy to understand and, learn, I believe, even by children who are closer to feeling and instincts. It explains all the factors about us humans, as I have attempted to explain in this book. The ramifications (implications) I feel would help us humans create a new course for life and living. Why it did not catch on initially was a surprise to me, but viewing the psychological profession and knowing the neurosis of mankind, it is not surprising that the profession claims it is too simplistic. The healthcare professionals are too vested in their complicated and sophisticated current system to give all that up. Stephen Hawking, in his book *A Brief History of Time*, suggests that if we discover Unified Field Theory, it would need to be simple and would need to be understandable by all of us and not just sophisticated physicists and mathematicians. If, as I have suggested, Primal Theory is Unified Field Theory, then it surely does fall into that category of being simple and universally understandable. The nature of the thinking mind is only part of the full-feeling process and all creatures, including ourselves, are creatures of feelings; alas, we have repressed almost all of ours.

I would like to summarize what I have written here and explain as best I can what Primal Therapy is about. Briefly; Primal Therapy is a therapy to *feel what feeling feelings feels like*. That may sound convoluted, but it is a complicated process; although Primal Theory is very simple, the practice of Primal Therapy is quite complex and can, in the hands of the uninitiated, be quite catastrophic. The Primal Institute and the Primal Center, both here in Los Angeles, state that it is very dangerous unless the therapist has been trained extensively at one of these institutions. Taking patients into old feelings that she/he is not ready for can initiate psychosis (as happened in some cases by using lysergic acid). Both the Primal Institute and the Primal Center require an extensive internship process to become a therapist. I fully concur with that. I have not been asked or trained to practice Primal Therapy

Neurosis is the problem. Neurosis is the pathology (death knell) of feelings. We need to relearn to feel, as best we can. Most of our preconceived ideas about many things need to be rethought. Maybe it is only youth, being close enough to their childhoods and feelings, who will grasp this. Can we collectively make a bold attempt to *not* damage our children as much as we were, thereby reducing neurosis in the next generation?

I wrote this to express myself in writing, to promote the theory that I felt was the outcome of the greatest discovery of all time and to encapsulate several divergent subjects under one heading and bring them together in one cause. Having promoted the ideas verbally over the years, I realized that most people over 25 had already become mature in their neurosis and it was hard to change their concepts unless their old feelings were rising and their defense system was weak. I therefore dedicate this to the children of the world and hope the youth, being closer to their feelings than most, might read it and get the "wow" factor. It was a long and arduous process over a period of more than 20 years of taking notes and trying out my ideas and opinions (feelings) verbally in the hope that I might see a way to write and be convincing.

Primal Therapy is not advisable for everyone, unless you really feel you have no other choice. However, as a species we can greatly benefit from knowing the theory and, hopefully, start a process whereby the next generation need not be as damaged as we are so that progressively (maybe in only four or five generations) all could become free from this extremely debilitating disease that causes 99% of the horrors of this world.

Jack's gospel in brief:

1) Neurosis is 99% of all our problems.

2) Feelings are everything; all else is irrelevant.

3) Thinking, without connecting it to the feeling that creates it, is neurotic.

4) Our cultures are our self-made prisons where we incarcerated ourselves.

5) Civilization is our curse, not our redemption.

6) Learning is simple; teaching is complicated and convoluted.

7) Once the problem is truly defined, it's simple. It's the solution that is complicated.

8) Economics is the quagmire which entrapped us.

9) "Free market practices" is an oximoran. It is anything but free.

10) Religion (believing) is the root of all evil, not the love of money.

11) To go from rules to laws, then laws to politics, then politics to money, is crazy.

12) Politicians don't have answers, only egos.

13) I feel, therefore I be (exist).

14) Childrearing is slavery: potential parents should fully understand this hardship.

15) Life's about experiencing it—billions of moments—just like now.

Glossary of Terms

Act-in: The body's attempt to do the same as the defense system and hide from pain by ultimately creating an illness to circumvent pain—a paradox.

Act-out: An action or ingestion (drugs) to defend against a rising feeling, known also as a defense.

Buddying: Two people getting together to listen to one another (one at a time) to express their feelings and thoughts on matters concerning the speaker.

Buddy: Someone who gets into buddying with you from time to time.

Center of the Cyclone: A philosophical book title by John C. Lilly suggesting that thinkers both spiritual and otherwise all headed towards a central point but that none of them seemingly, getting to that central point.

Dumping: In short, blaming others for our feelings, e.g. the boss gives you a bad time and you come home and kick the dog—a dump.

Etymology: The study of the origins or derivation of words from parent languages.

Foolscap: A British term for a piece of lined paper (sometimes yellow like legal pads).

Overwhelming pain: While it may seem obvious what the word "overwhelming" or the word "pain" mean, it is only when experiencing "overwhelming pain" we feel the gravity of it. The phrase almost defies explanation.

Primal: I use this in the context of "first" experiences (reliving) of feelings at the onset of our individual lives.

Primal Pain: Overwhelming pain laid down in our subconscious at a time of our early development from fetus to the end of childhood.

Reliving: Re-experiencing an event, normally painful, as it was at the time it actually occurred, as opposed to remembering that event.

Sovereign unto ourselves: Being our own personal authority unto ourselves.

Subliminal: One's awareness that there is something, but not quite having full knowledge or access to it—below the threshold of consciousness

Bibliography

The Primal Scream G. P. Putnam's Sons, 1970 by Dr. Arthur Janov

Prisoner of Pain Doubleday Press, 1980 by Dr. Arthur Janov

Why You Get Sick How You Get Well Dove Books, 1996 by Dr. Arthur Janov

Primal Healing New Page Books, 2006 by Dr. Arthur Janov

Cows, Pigs, Wars and Witches Random House, 1974 by Marvin Harris

Summerhill Hart Publishing Company, 1960 by A. S. Neill

A Brief History of Time Bantam Books, 1988 by Stephen W. Hawking

Seven Laws of Money Random House, 1974 by Michael Phillips

Das Kapital Verlag van Otto Meissner 1867 by Karl Marx

Birth Without Violences Newmarket Press 1990 by Dr. Frédérick LeBoyer

Continuum Concept Perseus, 1977 by Jean Liedloff

Real Fatherhood 1st Books Library, 2002 by Bob Kamm

The X-Rated Bible Feral House, 1998 by Ben Edward Akerley

Center of the Cyclone New York Julian Press, 1972 by John C. Lilly

Language, Thought, and Reality, Selected Writings of Benjamin Lee Whorf M. L. T. Press, 1956 by John B. Carroll

Index

A

B

C

D